CAN I SPEAK to SOMEONE in CHARGE?

EMILY CLARKSON

**SIMON &
SCHUSTER**

London · New York · Sydney · Toronto · New Delhi

A CBS COMPANY

First published in Great Britain by Simon & Schuster UK Ltd, 2017
A CBS COMPANY

Copyright © 2017 by Emily Clarkson

1 3 5 7 9 10 8 6 4 2

Simon & Schuster UK Ltd
1st Floor
222 Gray's Inn Road
London WC1X 8HB

www.simonandschuster.co.uk
www.simonandschuster.com.au
www.simonandschuster.co.in

Simon & Schuster Australia, Sydney
Simon & Schuster India, New Delhi

The author and publishers have made all reasonable efforts
to contact copyright-holders for permission, and apologise
for any omissions or errors in the form of credits given.
Corrections may be made to future printings.

A CIP catalogue record for this book
is available from the British Library

Paperback ISBN: 978-1-4711-5690-8
eBook ISBN: 978-1-4711-5691-5

Typeset in Bembo by M Rules
Printed and bound by CPI Group (UK) Ltd, Croydon, CR0 4YY

Contents

Acknowledgements

I want to dedicate this book to the lovely readers of Pretty Normal Me. I'm well aware that without your unwavering support I would be nothing and this book would not exist. I love you all so much.

I also need to thank my incredible boyfriend who has supported me down this path even though the destination has at times looked dubious. My dad, who inspires me to work harder and be a better writer. My friends, who never let me give up. And mostly, my wonderful mum whose love and support means more to me than she will ever know.

Dear You, Lovely Reader

Hello! Oh lordy, you've bought my book. I cannot believe it. Thank you. This means a lot to me. This is my first time, so I'm a little nervous; be gentle with me. It's so nice to have you here and I've honestly found myself a bit lost for words (just what you don't want to see written on the first page of a book, eh?).

Welcome to *Can I Speak To Someone In Charge?* I never normally read the preface of a book, but just in case you're a better person than I am, with more patience, let me tell you a little bit more about me, the blog and this book. The first thing I'd like you to know is that I consider myself to be a very normal girl. As I write this I'm lying on a sofa in my house with my feet in a suitcase (because I haven't yet unpacked from a trip I got back from a week ago and the house is a mess) with no make-up on and my double chin out in force. I'm in my early twenties and I struggle, as lots of girls do, with the pressures of everyday life. Despite that, I am inherently very happy. I love life, although I don't claim to understand it; the idea of space and time and nature and breathing and science and love confuse and terrify me in equal measure. I consider my life to be a true blessing and I therefore wanted to do something great with it. So I started my blog, Pretty Normal Me.

Pretty Normal Me began first as a hobby in November 2014, as I began to notice that the world around me somehow wasn't quite *right*. We were living in virtual realities that we didn't really understand (social media); we were all different sizes but still being encouraged to dress like clones of one another, and a lot of us were actually quite unhappy but we weren't sure why. The catalyst for me was an online shopping attempt, when I noticed there were lots of companies not stocking clothes bigger than a size 12. Once my eyes were opened to the problem I couldn't then close them again. From that point on I started seeing problems everywhere, not just in the fashion industry but in everything we did, from school to sport to parenting to washing our hair.

So I created a space where I hoped women would be able to come and celebrate themselves. Where they could be a bit squishy and be cool with it; where they could read something they were genuinely interested in and absolutely not have to feel guilty in any way, shape or form about the share box of doughnuts they'd just eaten; where they could be reminded that their lives were for living and that it was much too short to be spent counting calories, crying in Topshop or screaming at the scales.

I realised that being a 'normal girl' had become a near-impossible task, so I wanted to create a space that would inject a bit of normality back into the world. I wanted to remind my readers that it is OK not to be OK all the time. It's OK to have fun, to snort when you laugh, to wobble when you walk, wobble when you talk; it's OK to name your second chin, to get spots, to be fat, to be thin, to be sad, and it's OK to be weird.

As the blog grew I also wanted it to be a place where women could support one another and be supported in return, and I'm very excited as I think this is beginning to happen. There is a LOT of pressure on women right now and this was starting to worry me. I realised all of us were so much stronger when we stood together and I thought I would try to create a platform from which we would be able to do that. Well, ta-daa – three years later, here we are.

'Just imagine if we, the normal girls, stood united as an enormous, hysterical and proud army, we would be unstoppable!' This was the very first thing I wrote on Pretty Normal Me.

So now I've written a book, and I honestly cannot believe it. When I say I started Pretty Normal Me as a hobby, I really mean it; it was never supposed to be anything more than a passion project, a labour of love. And for a long time that is exactly what it was. I did it in my free time for no money with no one but my dog for company. But then I got really, really lucky and some lovely readers found me and supported me until, one day in June 2015, a lady called Abbie, an editor at Simon & Schuster, sent me an email (which I for sure thought was a prank) asking me if I had ever considered writing a book. (I had, by the way, in distant, far-off dreams I'd had as a child, which I never, ever, ever thought in a million years would come true.) Unsurprisingly I said yes and, with her help, and more recently, after her departure from S&S,

the help of lovely Nicki, I have written one. (When I say
I can't believe it I'm not exaggerating.) Thanks also to my
amazing, hard-working agent Becky and the rest of the
fabulous team at S&S, Jess, Justine and Rich!

And now you've bought it (or stolen it) and you're reading
it, and that makes me happier than I can tell you. Thank you
so much. So what can you expect? Well, if the front cover
didn't give it away, I'll explain: this book is a collection of
open letters. Although the blog was started initially as a
reaction to the fashion industry, there are, as I said, lots of
issues affecting women today and, to be honest, I thought it
was high time that someone called bullshit on them. So here
I am, screaming bullshit at the top of my lungs. At times
I get a little ranty, at times you might lose me in a train of
thought (I have a tendency to both speak and write exactly
what is on my mind at any given time), but I hope you will
get the gist of it.

But more than that, I hope this book helps you. I hope
you read it and have moments of 'Oh, thank fuck for that',
when you realise that you are not on your own in ripping
garments of clothing in shop changing rooms and farting in
the gym, because I can't be the only one that lives for those
reassurances. I hope you read it and laugh, whether that's at
me or with me, because laughter is the best medicine. And I
hope more than anything that you are able to take something
from it, whether that's something you can draw on when
you're feeling low, or something that inspires you to speak
up and fight for what you believe in, whatever that may be.

Despite the fact that we live online now and are never

further than a charged phone away from the outside world,
I know I'm not alone in feeling lonely from time to time.
I'm grateful to my wonderful friends and family but there
are some things I can't talk to them about, simply because I
haven't got the words with which to do it. And so I hope in
some way this book helps you feel less alone. Less vulnerable
and embarrassed and less like the only one in the world,
because you're not. I hope this book helps you to remember
that in some capacity. I also hope it opens your eyes to some
of the injustices women are facing right now, and some of
the areas in which the world is going wrong, so that when
the time comes to stand up and fight, we'll be ready to do it,
together.

Now, rather counterintuitively, I am actually writing
this letter last and, true to form, am running late with it,
so I have to go. Not least because today is deadline day and
the whole thing is becoming very real and I think I might
need a minute to myself to go and freak the fuck out. So
I'm going to leave you now – leave you to the passionate
opinions of someone who is so, so grateful to have you here.
Who doesn't know you, but who adores you. Of someone
who thinks that you are absolutely wonderful and perfect
and great and who doesn't think you should ever, ever
change, ever.

So much love to you all, enjoy!

Em xxxx

Dear Emily Aged Thirteen

Oh my gosh, darling one. Hi, how are you? Look, don't freak out or anything but this message is coming to you from the future. I'm twenty-three now and there is so much I wish I'd known at thirteen and so, just in case you're reading this, and we're able to completely fuck up the writing of history and everything that I believed to be true, I'm here to let you know that everything is going to be OK.

Now, first things first: you ought to know that blue eye-shadow has never worked for you and you'd do well to throw it away immediately. I know it's the only colour you've got, but you're going to need to work that out, because you look ridiculous. No arguments. Bin it, NOW.

Denim skirts are going to go out of fashion (they will come back in, so don't throw them out). Thankfully so will UGG boots, big elastic belts, all tie-dye prints, wearing leggings as trousers, kitten heels and the 'formal' dresses that go down to your knees that Mum keeps finding. (They don't come back in. Burn them, burn them now.)

Your hair. PLEASE STEP AWAY FROM YOUR HAIR. The natural colour is lovely (from what I can remember), although I suppose I'm too late and, by the time you'll be reading this, Becky will have already helped you to make it that weird orange colour. STOP THERE. In a few months you're going to try and fix it and it's going to go wrong, really wrong; it's going to go purple and Mum is going to go ballistic. Oh, and when you turn sixteen you're going to want to cut it all off. PLEASE DON'T DO THAT. Your head is much too big to pull off something like that. I regret it so much and it took ages to grow back. Just leave it alone.

Now, I know Facebook is very new and exciting but for the love of God stop writing on everybody's 'walls', stop telling them you love them, telling them secrets publicly, and please stop talking in abbreviations – it's not that hard to type the whole bloody word. You have an education; utilise it. With that in mind, please stop using a 'z' instead of an 's'; it's weird as fuck. In a few years, Facebook is going to start showing you posts from years ago and you're going to hate yourself for being so hopelessly uncool. If you want to talk to someone, text them; the limit on your phone allowing only twenty texts per month is going to be lifted very soon.

For the same reason it's probably a good idea to start smiling in photos. STOP POUTING. You look absolutely ridiculous and it means that whenever I try and get sentimental over my childhood I can't because I look like a moron in every single photo. Your braces aren't that bad and they're not going to stay on forever; in fact, at the end of this year you're going to BEG the orthodontist to take them off and, despite his better judgement, he will. If you can, please hang in there because, as a result of that decision, I still have a terrible overbite.

Oh yeah . . . and also, you know that pink pencil you've been putting on your eyes every morning? It's lip liner.

Now, down to more serious stuff: you ought to know
that you're going to get an ACTUAL boyfriend. I won't tell
you when because that'll ruin the surprise but, trust me, it's
going to happen. He's not going to ask you out over email
and it will last longer than four minutes; it's going to be the
real bloody deal. You're going to love him to bits and he's
going to catch you totally by surprise; he's going to tell you
he loves you one day and ask you to move in with him . . .
don't whatever you do freak out, it's going to be great.

That said, you need to prepare yourself for the fact that
you're going to make so many catastrophic mistakes in the
interim and there's nothing I can do to stop you. That would
take away all the fun and you wouldn't learn anything, but
it's worth you knowing that it's going to be fine. Where you
can, stop stressing about boys and relying on those stupid
algorithms you and your friends are making on scrap paper
in the back of the classroom to predict your future – they
don't know shit and, when it's meant to happen, it will.

I reckon your first kiss is just about due any day now,
actually, so try and enjoy that and don't be too nervous.
Over the next few years some of the boys you're going to
cross paths with are going to hurt you and make you sad. If
they're doing that then you need to know they are NOT the
one. Although you'll get confused, so confused, love does
not have to hurt; in fact it's going to do the opposite – it's
going to make your heart sing (yes, you DO grow up to be
this cheesy). You'd do well to remember that, and it'll also
mean that when the right guy shows up you'll know who
he is because you'll feel happy in yourself. You won't try to

change a million different things, you won't always need to look your best, and you will be so happy just being you.

You're also going to embarrass yourself in front of many a man – don't panic. It'll be mortifying, I won't deny it, but one day it'll be a distant memory. Roll with the discrepancies. Although they'll feel like hell at the time, they'll shape you into who you need to be. You are going to try to change yourself so many times and, at the risk of sounding like our mother, you're going to show off. I can't stop you, so do what you've got to do but just don't take anything too seriously.

I know you know this already, and you're going to cringe as you read it, but it's got to be said: you are going to be so grateful for any male attention for the next few years but that's so wrong. I don't want to throw the big scary words around, but a lot of the messages you'll start receiving on Facebook Messenger are going to be borderline sexual harassment. The worst part about this is you're going to go along with it rather than speak up for yourself. In fact, you're going to get oddly excited by it all but you don't need to do this. This is not the kind of attention you want; you deserve more, remember that.

You just need to remember to respect yourself, and that you're not 'frigid' if you don't want to send a photo to a guy – you're sensible. And I know that's not what you want to be right now but trust me – it's so much better than the alternative. Boys have just started watching porn and, because they're a bit weird right now, they're going to assume they can treat girls how they like, but they will grow out of it. I know it makes you uncomfortable when they talk about it in front of you and that's OK. Don't feel like you need to laugh along in order to fit into the preconceived ideas they have for you; you will never be that person and I don't want you wasting a whole heap of time trying to fit that mould.

But actually, and I'm sorry to say, it's not just the boys you need to worry about. More so than them it's the girls that are going to cause the problems. This is something I know you suspect already, although you won't admit it for a while, but I'm serious. You need to start worrying, and fast.

Girls, I'm afraid, are inherently mean creatures. You are too – we can't help it. Particularly for the next few years it's going to be a relentless stream of passive-aggressive bitchiness all wound up into a little ball of competition and hugs. There are so many times when you're going to think you're doing something for the boys – wearing something for that one guy in particular – and although of course there is an element of that, most of your insecurity here is going to come about as a result of other girls, and you will, in turn, start making the effort for them. I can't stop you, and unfortunately it's not going to go away, but you might as well know about it.

Girls are going to say things over the next few years completely by accident, without thinking anything of it or even trying to be rude, that are going to stay with you for years and years to come. I wish you had thicker skin, and I wish I could tell you this was all going to be water off a duck's back but, I'm really sorry, some of it is going to

stick. I'm just giving you some warning. They don't mean
to be bitches, most of them; it's a dog-eat-dog world out
there for a girl and I'm afraid that's the way it has to be for a
while. Don't take it personally. That said, don't bite back . . .
never bite back. It's not worth causing someone else years of
insecurities just because you feel embarrassed and victimised.
Some of my biggest regrets are offhand comments I've made
to people, which I'm well aware if the tables were turned
would still be upsetting me today.

The whole sex thing is important here too, as it's as much
to do with girls as it is with boys right now. Please spread the
message far and wide: it is NOT a competition. Never feel
like you need to do something because your friends have.
In the grand scheme of life no one cares who the first fella
was who felt you up. You don't need to tell people when
it happens. Everything you do should be because YOU
want to; not because the girl you sit next to in English has.
I promise you this: sex will not make you a better person,
it will not make you more mature, and you'd do well to
remember that every other girl out there is just as scared as
you right now. Please, please respect yourself.

The other thing you need to know is that over the next
five years you are going to be told by anyone who has even
sensed a grey hair coming on that 'your school years are the
best of your life'. I have to say, unless it all goes incredibly,
drastically downhill from where I am now, this is absolute
horseshit.

There will of course be elements of school that are
amazing. Memories will be made that will last a lifetime

and you will have so much fun. Having said that, though, you will also have some really shitty times and, I promise you, since leaving school they are much fewer and further between. I now get to wear whatever I want EVERY DAY, I don't have someone okaying the length of my skirt before I go to a party (although if it's really short enough that it needs to be 'okayed' then it is definitely too short), I can eat what I want, whenever I'm hungry, I can stay out as late as I like and I can even smoke now. Although, please, for the love of all that is good, when Georgie takes you into the bushes in a couple of months and offers you your first cigarette, SAY NO. Apart from the obvious health stuff it's a bastard to give up and is costing me a fortune.

There is SO much I want to tell you. I get a stabbing pain in my stomach as I write this because I'm so bitterly aware of the anguish you're going to go through. When you're feeling sad, don't go it alone. I have memories of crying myself to sleep. I can still feel my cheeks burning when I remember feeling uncomfortable around people I didn't know that well, and I vividly remember the heartbreak that comes with feeling like you don't belong.

If I could swap with you I would; I would do so many things differently. I'd say no to that first cigarette. I'd establish myself early on with friends who love me for me. I'd stop trying so hard. I'd leave my hair alone. I'd throw out those horrible green tracksuit bottoms you wear all the time but, most importantly, I would try really hard to be happy.

Because I wasted *so* much time not being, and I regret it so much.

All I can tell you is that it's going to get easier. I promise you, every day will be easier than the last. There is so much I'd change, of course there is, but I know you and I know that you're as stubborn as fuck, and so I'm pissing in the wind by even asking. But if there is one thing I need you to start doing, it is practising self-love. From time to time, please, try it for me. Look in the mirror, find something good and hold onto it. Look back at your day, your week, and find something you did that you're proud of. Be kind to yourself, rest and have fun. You've got a very big heart and you need to make room in there for you. Please, do that for me. I promise the moment you do your life will get so, so much better.

The next few years are going to be an obstacle course and by the time you get to the finish line you are going to be absolutely knackered, but it's one hell of a race and you will get there stronger and better than you ever thought you would.

I'll be waiting for you when you get through it, with a massive glass of wine and a cigarette, because, let's face it – you're definitely not going to say no to that first one.

Good luck, little me, see you on the other side.

Em x

Dear School

cc All headteachers, PSHE teachers, people who organise the menus, exam boards, the teacher that told me that I'd get a D in my GCSE English exam

Hi, sorry I'm late. Mr Smith's class ran over and I literally had to run here. (Translation: I overslept during my free period and, if I'm honest, I totally forgot we had a lesson. I know you know that, but thank you very much for playing along with my little charade.) Anyway, I'm here now. What did I miss?

You know, everyone who is anyone tells me that their school years were the best of their lives. Literally, I hear it everywhere. When I was at school and my parents would drag me to grown-up parties, it would be the default line; the patronising ponderings of someone resenting their mortgage, their bosses and the fact that they just found a grey pube. I know that if I so much as thought about complaining about a deadline or a teacher then I would be met with the inevitable: 'Oh, you think that YOU'RE stressed, do you? Just you wait, Missy, just you wait. What I wouldn't give to be back at school . . .' And then they would tumble into nostalgic ramblings of 'simpler' times before the ever-predicable: 'You know, they were the best days of my life, my school days.' But if I'm honest – and no offence here – I just don't *get* that at all.

If I'm going to tell you the truth, which I suppose I probably ought to, I ought to admit that I'm not even sure I liked school very much. Looking back, although I can remember having fun, more than anything I feel this discomfort in my stomach like a ball of tension when I think about it. All of my memories are somehow tarnished with a brush dipped in this cauldron of uncertainty and, actually, if I think about it really hard, my discomfort becomes comparable to one of those big balls you used to make out of elastic bands – too tight and ready to snap at any minute.

I remember my cheeks burning red every single time my teachers asked me to answer a question. I remember feeling in the way quite a lot but, more than anything, I remember convincing not only myself but anyone around me that I was incredibly happy and comfortable at school. Which is kind of weird when you take into consideration the fact that at times school was actually quite horrid, that I never *really* felt that I fitted in; that I was never the cleverest or the prettiest or the best. That my uniform never fitted properly, my exam results were never great, that I felt constantly on edge among my friends, as if they would smell me for the fake I was and drop me. But do you know why that is? Why I basically lived a lie for fifteen years? It's because you, school, were SO DAMN STRESSFUL.

It starts early, the stress. Aged whatever and you're in Clarks doing your uniform shopping. AND OH MY GOD WHY ARE THERE SO MANY OPTIONS OF SHOE? What's everyone else wearing? Laces surely? Velcro is just for kids. NO MUM NO I DON'T CARE HOW SUPPORTIVE THEY

ARE THEY'RE JUST NOT COOL. Queue the tears. Shit, did that girl in the year above me just see me crying? I CAN NEVER GO BACK TO SCHOOL AGAIN. I want to die. MUM, you're SO embarrassing. STOP TALKING TO ME. Yes, I'm sure I want these ones. Are you kidding me? I don't need to walk BOTH lengths of the shop. I know they fit FINE ... I won't regret it, they're my feet and YOU DON'T KNOW ANYTHING. They're just what's cool right now and I wouldn't expect you to understand anyway.

Then there's the first day stress. OH MY GOD MY FILE IS TOO PINK. I knew it. Why didn't I get the black one? See, Mum. WHY DID YOU MAKE ME GET THE PINK ONE? Pink isn't cool anymore. Oh, my God, does no one use pencil cases anymore? Where are everyone's pencil cases? Where are they keeping their pens? Maybe pens aren't cool anymore. Is that possible? WHY DID NO ONE TELL ME? MUM KEEP THIS PENCIL CASE IN THE CAR DON'T LOOK UP JUST DRIVE DRIIIIIIIIVE!

Then I'm in the classroom and this dickhead teacher thinks he's being cool by not giving us assigned seats. You're NOT being cool. I hate you for this. What if no one chooses me? They're not going to. Fuck, I'm going to be on my own. OK. Act like you don't care. Just sit down now and play with something to distract you. SHIT I LEFT MY PENCIL CASE IN THE CAR AND MOBILE PHONES AREN'T A THING YET SO I HAVE NOTHING TO DO. OK. Stop blushing. They can smell fear. SWALLOW IT EM, THEY WON'T SIT NEXT TO A WEAKLING. Am I on my own? Has anyone chosen me? Oh, thank God for that. Please let these be our seats forever now. I can't do this again. Wait . . . what do you mean we're moving classrooms? I can't. I'm never leaving this desk again. And you, my desk friend, you aren't going anywhere either. SIT DOWN.

Now it's break time. I have no gossip. Nothing to offer. Who in their right mind is going to care that I spent a huge portion of my summer collecting woodlice with my sister? They've all been having sleepovers and going on dates. How does that even happen? Why wasn't I invited to these sleepovers or asked on dates? How do you even find someone who will ask you on a date? Well, no one will ask me when they realise my hobbies consist of nothing more than catching woodlice with my sister anyway, so it's all irrelevant. I can't handle twenty-five minutes of this. Ooh yummy! Custard creams. Love custard creams. Is it OK to eat biscuits? Is that cool? It frigging better be 'cos I'm starving and it's been at least three hours since I've eaten anything. That won't do. I'm a growing girl, after all. I'll just watch for a bit . . . yup, OK, that's a fair few girls in the queue now, I'll go.

Wait, what do you mean we have our clothes test today? We've got to go SWIMMING? IN OUR CLOTHES? AND COLLECT A BRICK FROM THE BOTTOM OF THE POOL? WITH BOYS? I'VE EATEN TWELVE FUCKING CUSTARD CREAMS. SURELY I'M GOING TO DROWN. Shit. Shit shit shit shit. Why didn't they tell me? My PE kit is white. It's going to go see-through. Should I be wearing this crop-top? Is it cool? What's everyone else wearing? Bras? I bet they are. I bet their mums have taken them bra shopping because they've hit puberty, lucky shits. That at least explains the dates. OK, so I'm wearing a crop-top, that can't be bad, can it? It's weird to check, isn't it? But hang on . . . if I stand behind this girl I might be able to see down the back of her top? No, abort mission, abort mission. She saw. FUCK. Now I look like a terrible creep. Oh God, I'm so embarrassed. THE WHOLE THING IS JUST SO STUPID. When would I EVER need to know how to swim with my clothes on anyway? I hate this. I can't do it.

Now it's Friday and everyone's having a sleepover. Am I going to be allowed to go? How do I put this to my parents? I'll tell them that I NEEEEEED to go. It's true. Imagine everything I'll miss. Can't afford not to go. But hang on, did they say were going to watch *IT* – the film with the killer clown? I hate clowns so much. Yup, that's that, I'm never sleeping again. Did everyone else find it scary? I'm never going to be able to shower again (fifteen years later and I'm still scared to shower). What if I talk in my sleep? Oh God, is it really tragic that I want to go home? I'm so hungry; why is no one eating that delicious-looking pizza? Well, someone needs to eat the last piece, for God's sake. I'll do it. And this mattress is so uncomfortable and why are we talking about boys all the time? I literally have nothing to offer to this. But I can't be the first to fall asleep. Rule one of sleepovers: NEVER BE THE FIRST TO FALL ASLEEP.

★ ★ ★

Fast forward a few years and it's time for big school. I'm allowed to wear MAKE-UP? Get out of town. I've got my mobile phone, my NEW uniform and I'm ready. Wait, am I the only one still wearing braces? I can't be. Oh no, please no, I need these off NOW. Brace face, metal mouth. I cannot take this; no one will ever snog me as long as I look like this. And wait, is that huge sparkly sack in that girl's bag a MAKE-UP BAG? It's huge! How does she have so much stuff? Where does she put it all? And where did she learn how to do it? Oh, my God, I can't deal with this. Literally that's so much make-up . . . why don't I have that? Did she buy it all with her pocket money or has she just got a really cool mum? Don't ask, be nonchalant about it.

Oh great. Another school where pencil cases aren't cool. WHEN DID THIS BECOME A THING? I haven't got space in my pocket for a protractor. This is ridiculous. RIGHT, I'm going to need to make it work somehow. This jacket is WAY too big. What was Mum thinking? I haven't grown for a year and there is no way I'm going to grow INTO this. WHY ARE EVERYONE ELSE'S PARENTS SO COOL?

OK, so I've been invited to a party on Saturday night. That is UNBELIEVABLE. I'm so excited. What am I going to wear? Well, it's 2007 and my first opportunity to wear high heels, so let's make some terrible fashion decisions. Backcombing is cool, right? People do that? And denim skirts? And my £4 red New Look high heels? And this PINK top? With this blue eye-shadow? And this silver lip-gloss? To go with this gold belt? Yes. Now whatever you do DON'T SMILE. Act like you don't care, like you do this all the time. Do I want some vodka? No, not really. DON'T ADMIT THAT. SAY YES. DRINK THE VODKA. IT'S COOL.

OH CRAP. We've been caught smuggling it into school. What teacher thinks to check a shampoo bottle for vodka? My parents are going to kill me. Ah. They're mostly worried about the risk of drinking shampoo. Will they ever get over this? (On the bright side, this is great for my street cred.)

And then, before you know it, it's exam time. And bam! These exams are going to shape the REST OF YOUR LIFE. THEY DETERMINE EVERYTHING ABOUT YOU. THEY MEASURE YOUR FUTURE SUCCESS. NO PRESSURE BUT YOUR ENTIRE LIFE IS RIDING ON THIS PIECE OF PAPER. But don't work too hard or you'll be a nerd who never has any friends or does anything cool. Act like you don't care. But don't come across as stupid because people don't like that and that's not cool either. I think clever is cool but too clever isn't, so walk that line well. This is ridiculous, why can't I live in New York? I've been watching *Gossip Girl* for a whole month now and those kids never seem to do any work, yet they're all top of their class and really, really clever. Another reason why I just want to be Serena van der Woodsen ... SHE is smashing life and smashing school. Why isn't my school like that? I would LOVE that life.

★ ★ ★

Jesus Christ. Pause for air. I just wrote that so fast my fingers are hot and that ball of tension in my stomach has grown so big it's now stuck somewhere in my throat. Who knew it could still stress me out so much however many years later? Even the thought of it is making me nervous.

And you know what? This stress, although seemingly

nothing but a hysterical nightmare to me, is actually causing some fairly serious issues. Actually, scrap the fairly, it's causing fucking pandemonium. School is the birthplace for so much shit: eating disorders, insecurities, anxiety and depression, to name but a few. God knows it's not deliberate on your part and you're not going out of your way to cause these problems but, let's face it, you're not doing nearly enough to stop them either.

Everything is shit when you're a teenager. It's just one of those things. But then you couple that with the fact that we are encouraged to be clones of one another, that being different is the worst thing ever, that we all have to wear the same clothes every day, that we are literally ranked in order of stupidity in classrooms and that all of those hormones and insecurities meet once a day in a cafeteria ... it's a recipe for unmitigated disaster. The charity Ditch the Label found in 2016 that 50 per cent of young people, 1.5 million, had been bullied in the previous year and, of those, 145,800 young people had been bullied EVERY DAY. That's a LOT of misery, guys. More worrying still, 44 per cent of young people who have been bullied are experiencing depression and 33 per cent of those being bullied have had suicidal thoughts. But the MOST worrying thing about all of this is that 45 per cent of the young people bullied in the previous year told the charity they didn't feel the school or college was taking the issue seriously enough. It's a shambles.

There isn't even a little bit of me that would be happy to send my daughter into the clutches of a school right now. Although I'd argue that education is THE most important thing a person can have, the fact is I don't think school is a very safe place for children anymore. It feels like a wolf in sheep's clothes – something we should be very frightened of but are for some reason approaching daily.

Yes, at the end of the day, a lot of this misery is a result of behavioural problems, and I know that kids pick up a lot at home, but really, this is happening on your watch. At all schools – private, grammar, comp, it doesn't matter – this is a nationwide epidemic. Looking at the statistics it's a miracle any of us makes it out at all, and for something that's a legal requirement and takes up a quarter of a person's life, this is something I'm not sure is even close to good enough. And that's a conversation we need to have. Well, it's just one of them, because education is a gift and school should be a privilege, but at the moment it feels to so many like a punishment.

But while I have you here I would also like to talk about the fact that even though your SOLE purpose was to set me up for life, I left at the age of eighteen basically clueless. Although I appreciate being able to list the names and fates of Henry VIII's six wives, I am left scratching my head when it comes to the common sense stuff. Here is some of the stuff I didn't know, that I definitely should have known, when I left school:

- How to read the label on clothes to know what temperature they should be washed at.
- That knives shouldn't go in the dishwasher.
- How to cook anything other than mac and cheese.

- How to use any gym equipment.
- What council tax is.
- How to pay taxes.
- What exactly a credit card is and how it works.
- That there was another type of contraception that wasn't a condom.
- To know that I should never take out a loan.
- How to sew on a button.
- How to wire a plug.
- How to iron a shirt.
- How to change a tyre.

And if I'm honest that's not even scratching the surface. I left school TOTALLY ill-equipped for real life, surrounded by some pretty miserable people. I was overweight with absolutely no idea how to cook anything other than frozen pizza (it says it on the packet) and cheesy pasta (because my mum taught me) or what exercise I should be doing or how I would even start doing it. I had no CV and no idea how to make one and I actually left with four A-Levels that no one, and I mean no one, has ever asked me about. And seeing as a fair old chunk of my life thus far (three quarters) was spent in education, I'm actually a little bit pissed off. I know you're trying your best, I understand you're stretched unbelievably thin, and I get that you don't really know what to do, but we are going to have to work something out.

Don't get me wrong, I did have some fun at school, but I ought to confess that I never felt I was being myself; I never felt comfortable enough for that. So while there are lots of

memories I can look back on and smile at, a lot of them don't
even feel like mine. School IS easy for some people, and
those are the ones, I now realise, who say their school days
are, or were, the best of their lives. Their hair fell just right
and their uniform looked good and they were the perfect
balance of clever and cool. But the rest of us weren't very
good and we didn't find it easy at all. Nor did we find help
or guidance in any capacity. Is it because we are just statistics
now, or is it because the issues are so prevalent that you are
stretched to bursting point?

I really don't know what the answer is, but I do know
that you needed to hear all of this. You need to know that
for a lot of us school really was the worst, and you also need
to know, while I'm here, that it's high time the syllabus got
updated: it's time to teach kids how the country is led so
that when they reach eighteen and are able to vote they can
make informed and educated decisions. It's time to teach
kids about activism so they can grow up as feminists and
gay rights campaigners and work to create a better, more
humane world. It's time to teach them how to live in the
world of today without just spitting them out in June of
their final year and wishing them well. They say children
are the future, which is, of course, the truth. But what
does that mean for us now? For our future? For theirs?
Because all I can see now is carnage: knives in toasters,
twats in government and undercooked chicken ... that's
today's future and it's looking pretty bleak. Please guys, do
something.

Perhaps we could stop spending so much time looking for

X and chanting out dead languages and spend a little more time learning about the birds and the bees (from someone who wasn't around when rationing was still a thing). Perhaps we could focus on learning some actual proper life skills that will HELP us in the big wide world?

I was lost and confused when I left school and I'll be damned if I have to send my children into a life of stress, drama and, ultimately, misery.

See you at the ten-year reunion I suppose!

Em x

Dear The Person Who Catfished Me

I'm not going to use your real name for this letter although I do now know it, as for some reason I want to extend a courtesy of protection that I don't think you deserve. I can't bring myself to ruin your life, despite the fact that you turned mine totally upside down. For when you added me on Facebook nearly nine years ago, pretending to be an older boy I had gone to school with, you tore from me all the trust that I, at fifteen, should have had in people.

Do you remember how it started? I do, plain as day. But everything that happened afterwards I have locked away in a part of my brain I cannot find the key for. It holds all the memories I wish to forget – the ones I'm ashamed of and can't talk about. It's as if it never happened, the friendship and excitement and, later, the fear and betrayal – gone. I had to ring my mum and rehash the whole traumatising thing with her, just to try and shine a light on this time of my life that is nothing more than a haze. I don't know how my brain has done this, how it has locked you out, but it has. I couldn't remember any of it.

But I will never forget how it started. I was sitting at the kitchen table on a family holiday in the Isle of Man. I was

at an age when any male attention was craved and I lived
for the moments when my BlackBerry would sing to life,
letting me know that someone was trying to contact me.
And there you were – a Facebook request from Eddie Speer,
along with a message. This was back in the days when 'no
mutual friends' wasn't suspicious, because being on the
same network was evidence enough, and somehow you had
squeezed your way onto my school network.

You were handsome, claiming to be nineteen and now
in the army, working as a Jack Wills model before you got
deployed and I, of course, accepted your friend request.
When I then received a long Facebook message from
you telling me you'd seen me at a carnival on the Isle of
Man earlier that week, and that you wanted to know how
everything at school was going, should I have been alarmed?
Should I have been suspicious? Probably. But I was fifteen
and insecure and you wanted to talk to little old me. You
asked me how I was, you asked me if the school still had the
same headmaster, and you used such familiar slang when
describing elements of the school that I really saw no red flag
or warning light. Or maybe I did and I just ignored it but,
either way, I replied.

Thus began our online friendship. It started off as
occasional messages, once a day maybe. What did we talk
about in the early days? I can't remember, but before I knew
it the messages were more and more regular. We had full-on
conversations; we spoke for hours and hours about what we
were both up to, about our lives. If I remember correctly,
at one point you even gave me your number. But we never

spoke on the phone; something I didn't think weird at the time. For some reason it never mattered that I hadn't met you in the flesh or even heard the sound of your voice; the constant stream of Facebook messages was more than enough for me – it was perfect. You'd tell me about things you'd been doing, walks you'd been on or parties you'd been to and, just like that, photos would appear on your timeline of you doing those very things. Why would I be suspicious of that?

I went to Corfu later that summer and still remember sitting on top of the WiFi box, waiting for messages from you. I remember staying up much too late every evening just talking to you. You told me so many things, so many stories that I believed to be true. You told me about films we had both watched, about your friends and family, about the time you were with your friend and had lost your car keys and had to walk all the way to the police station to see if they'd been handed in. Was it weird that in the story you'd been just outside my house in the Isle of Man? Yes, it probably was, but not to me. To me it was amazing – you were telling me everything, and I loved it.

As I try to unlock this part of my history, I remember meeting a friend for coffee when I got home and telling them all about you, my grown-up friend. My boyfriend? No, I mustn't get ahead of myself. You e-introduced me to your two best friends, a boy and a girl, about whom I'd heard so much, and I accepted their Facebook requests as soon as they came in. I felt like we were all forming an alliance. Was I naïve? Fuck, yes I was, but I was so caught up in it I didn't care.

When you told me you were being deployed to Iraq I
was worried. It was 2009 and that was not a safe place to
be, least of all as part of the British Army. I was so worried
that I opened up to my mum about it. I told her you were
to be deployed for six weeks which, to my mind, after we
had spoken every day, was a lifetime and I was heartbroken.
Little did I know that this was enough to cause the
alarm bells I couldn't hear to go off at full volume in my
mother's ears; no one went on tour for only six weeks, but
how was I to know? From time to time I would still get
messages from you, from Iraq, and you would tell me about
goings-on. As if! Looking back now, I was SO stupid for
believing that you could tell me what you were telling me
from a war zone but I didn't care – I was just so happy to
hear from you. And in my defence, when I went to check
the news after we'd spoken, I would see that these events
were really happening – just not to you.

Not telling me at the time, so as not to alarm me, my
mum trusted her intuition and decided to call the school,
asking if anyone by the name of Eddie Speer had ever
attended, to which she was told no, they hadn't. After
finding out that at least parts of the story I had been told
were not true, she then called the police – by this point
frightened – and they advised that she get me to disconnect
my Facebook page and let the whole thing rest. This wasn't
good enough for her, as I was in too deep, so she dug once
more and found a contact to talk to at the army itself, and
still I was none the wiser.

When she received the call telling her that not only

was there no one by the name of Eddie Speer currently
on operations in Iraq, but there was no one by that name
in the whole British Army, my mum finally told me. I'll
never forget this moment. I was in Bicester Village, in the
back of Paul Smith, trying on a blue-and-white-striped
blouse. A blouse I still have to this day and, although I
cannot wear it, I cannot bring myself to throw it away
either. It was as if my whole life had been turned on its
head.

How could I have been so stupid? So, so stupid – as if
someone as cool as you could ever really be interested in
overweight, frizzy-haired, insecure me! I couldn't believe
this. How did my mum know? How dare she go behind
my back? She was lying! It wasn't possible, was it? How
am I ever going to look anyone in the eye ever again? I
remember crying, I remember shaking, but most of all
I remember feeling so ashamed of myself. But if I felt
embarrassed now, it was nothing compared to what came
next.

Before I knew it we had a private investigator involved.
They got to work fairly quickly and it was all a bit of a
blur. I don't know if this is just part of what I've blanked
from my memory, or if my parents just didn't tell me all of
it to protect me, but I remember little of this time. Now
I don't think I would even recognise the PI if he slapped
me in the face, but I do remember having to hand over
my passwords and phone not only to a complete stranger,
but to my parents as well. During this time I couldn't look
any of them in the eye, which, thinking about it, might

have something to do with why I've blanked it from my memory. Having your parents read every excruciating detail of your life in the shape of hundreds of messages every day with a total stranger who, as it transpired, didn't even exist, was the worst thing that could have happened to me. And no, they weren't 'sexts', but to my mind, having poured my heart out, this was worse. It was at this point they tracked the IP address of your computer and found that you were not in Iraq; you were at a university.

As the private investigator and his team delved deeper, it was decided that CEOP (the Child Exploitation and Online Protection Centre) should get involved, and shit got weird. I had to have 'protection' at both school and home, in the form of someone watching me – I was told about this in the headmaster's office, and I just remember feeling so small in this big room surrounded by people from CEOP and my teachers. I had to have some weird policewoman come and see me at school to show me the ins and outs of my Facebook account and what I needed to do to protect myself, and I remember spending a day in Covent Garden with some of my friends, which was totally turned upside down when I saw that our now 'mutual friends' were posting photos from the same place as where I was.

This was back in the days of sharing every intricate detail of our lives on each other's Facebook walls. Rather than texting and wasting phone credit, we would write our plans and make arrangements very publically. So my plans were on my Facebook wall, in full view of you. Although

I'm not sure I actually posted all that much on my wall (surely I wasn't that stupid), there was nothing I could do about my friends writing what they wanted. I can't really remember anything we did that day, but nothing will take away the icy feeling I got when I looked on Facebook and saw that you were so close to me. I remember calling my parents in a panic; I remember being rushed to my friend's house in a taxi, and I remember my dad picking me up later that night. And that's it.

And since someone else had taken over being me in our friendship, I was therefore not to know that while I had been busy having every secret torn from me in the hunt for clues, you were still tapping away at your keyboard, living your own little virtual reality, and that you had actually killed Eddie off – that in this particular fantasy he had been blown up by an IED in Iraq and I was about to be invited up to your house to be comforted by his friend who, as it transpired, was you.

I don't remember where I was when I was told that the police had raided your student house in the northwest of England, but I remember what my mother said: 'Darling, the police have found the person who has been talking to you. They've arrested her.'

Her? Her?! I couldn't believe it. Up until this point the assumption had been that you were a paedophile, and after you got your 'friends' involved, that you might have even been part of a paedophile ring, but YOU – a twenty-year-old female student training to be a teacher? Somehow this was so much worse. I wanted to hate you so, so much for

what you did. But how could I, when we discovered that
your only motive was that you wanted to be my friend?
That you had seen me on the streets of the Isle of Man
and thought what a wonderful life I must lead, being the
daughter of a celebrity. And you know, the fact that the
whole thing was so tragic, so *innocent* . . . while it stops
me from hating you, it also prevents me from getting any
closure on the whole fucked-up thing.

I haven't thought about you in the last decade really,
although Mum has often tried to encourage me to speak
out about this at schools and to younger people in a bid to
ensure they protect themselves online, but I can't. Because
at the end of it all I was made sad by the whole situation.
I was stupid, I know that. I was naïve, I know that. But I
was also left bereft. Because regardless of the whole crazy
situation I actually lost a friend. I'm grateful that we never
pressed charges, I really am. And I'm sorry for you that as a
result of your actions you are now unable to teach children
but, if we're honest, that's probably for the best.

What I really can't forgive you for, though, is the fact
that you went into this thing lying and never even gave
me a chance. To this day I find it hard to trust people. I'm
constantly left wondering if people are really friends with
me for me, or if they just do it because I'm Jeremy Clarkson's
daughter and, after the lengths you went to, who can blame
me? At fifteen, I shouldn't have had to go through all of that,
and I shouldn't have had to have these doubts; I should have
just been happy being trusting. And I couldn't be after that,
and that's what I can't forgive you for.

Despite everything, though, I hope you've found happiness somehow, somewhere, and this period of your life is behind you. I hope you've found a way of existing in the real world and have realised that you, as a person, are enough.

Em

Dear Prosecco

Where the fuck do I start? Well, I suppose I ought to start with a little story. Not that long ago my friend Omey (trust me, you know her) and I went out for a quiet dinner. What happened afterwards was what led me to know with absolute certainty that it was going to be you, and you alone, that would be responsible for my undoing.

I had just finished work, my boyfriend was in New York, and I had nothing planned that night. On my way home Omey rang me and asked if I'd like to go to the pub for a quiet drink – another friend had had a tough day and was going to meet us for a quick one. That particular friend was drinking orange juice, but Omey and I thought that, since we had a packet of fags each and the weather was nice that evening, we might as well make the most of it, and ordered a bottle. By the time our friend had to leave, the bottle was gone and it was time for another. Next, Omey's father arrived by chance and we ended up having dinner with him, which was of course accompanied by another bottle and then, because we didn't have room for dessert but certainly weren't finished with our night, we ordered a fourth. By this point it was dark, and as responsible twenty-something-year-olds we probably ought to have known it was time to go home. But unsurprisingly, thanks to you, we'd totally forgotten how to be responsible anything-year-olds, and found ourselves following our feet in the direction of a good night out.

What happened next I'm pretty sure could, would – hell, SHOULD – make it as a sell-out sequel to *The Hangover*. Unsurprisingly my memory is hazy, but the next morning – covered in bruises and surrounded by sticky Jägerbomb residue – we pieced it back together. There was dancing, there was snogging and there was a HUGE wipe-out on the dancefloor of the club (Omey was not only responsible, but ended up on the bottom of it). There were strange men whom we accosted and insisted pay for our taxi, as we circled familiar streets looking for anywhere that might still be open; there was that soul-crushing moment when we bumped into Omey's ex-boyfriend, for whom I have as little respect as is possible. I told him as much (except a little less eloquently and with a few more C-bombs) and then there was more dancing. Before I knew it, Omey was gone (I would later discover she'd been put into a taxi by that twat and, at the other end, had opened the car door only to discover that her body no longer worked and, as she fell from seat to road, her hands did nothing to protect her face from the tarmac. By all accounts the tears could be heard four streets down) and I was dancing, literally, until I was the last person standing. I woke up on the sofa with my flatmate tapping me, fear in her eyes as she explained that she literally thought I was dead, still fully clothed and absolutely hammered.

But why am I telling you this? No one died, no one ate

a live bat or caught a squirrel or stole a pig. There was no
hospital trip, so what is the point, what is the significance
of this particular story? Well, there isn't any. I'm telling you
this story because it's a story we all know so well. It is the
story of my life. To my mind, it's not a night worth having
if you haven't been carried to bed via the service elevator by
five friends at your best friend's wedding, only to wake up
totally naked on an office chair in a strange hotel room with
a blinder of a bruise on your head and your boyfriend sitting
in the bath eating biscuits. (Last weekend.) It's how I spend
at least one night a week and have been doing for as long as
I can remember. I've got stories like these coming out of my
ears.

Like that time I had one too many glasses of something,
ate an entire watermelon in under a minute (a dare) and
proceeded to throw it all up over not only the pavement but
the people I had just proven wrong. Or one of the many
times that I lost my bank card and/or driving licence. Or the
time I snogged the bouncer. Or the time my boyfriend and I
spent half an hour haggling with the guy in Subway for 30p
off his foot-long, or the time I bruised two ribs falling off a
bench outside the pub, or the time I had to catch my friend's
vomit in a taxi on the way home from a club in Moscow,
pretending to the taxi driver that there was nothing to worry
about, while Charlie's vomit seeped through my fingers and
onto the carpet.

Or all the times I've been sick in places I absolutely
shouldn't have been sick in: like in the dishwasher, or the
sink, or the shower. Or the time I was sick out of a taxi

window and the time I was sick into a plastic bag filled with holes and thus created a sprinkler-type effect. There have been countless times when I've had to make a speedy dash to a club or office loo for a tactical chunder, and there have been times when they haven't been quite so tactical; like when, rather than projecting out of me, my vomit just sort of fell, slowly and unimpressively, down the front of my shirt.

Or what about all of those times I've woken up, either from a full night's sleep or a quick disco nap, somewhere that was absolutely not my intended resting spot . . . my sofa being a favourite, with my car a close second. There have been strange beds, flower beds, dog beds . . . any beds really, seemingly just never mine. There have been taxis, pavements, nightclubs and gym changing rooms. Not forgetting, of course, that one time I fell asleep upstairs in McDonald's, only to wake up in the pitch black with no one but a lonely and very startled cleaner for company.

These are all things that absolutely, categorically, would not be happening if it were not for you. But I'm not taking it personally, as I know it's not just me you're sabotaging. You seem hell-bent on taking my friends down with you too. I only had to think of the question before countless horror stories came tumbling out of everyone's mouths.

I've got friends who have been sick EVERYWHERE. Into their parents' glove compartments, in clear doggy bags and in another friend's shoes. I've got a friend who was so hungover she was sick all over the doorman's shoes at Harrods and who, on another occasion, was sick on a club

DJ. I've got friends who have been sick at the top of the stairs only to watch it project all the way down them. I've got a friend who was drunkenly sick off her hotel balcony one evening only to find the next morning that it had landed on the roof of next door's conservatory. I've got friends who have been sick in their shot glasses, onto their plates and onto railway lines. I have a friend who sent me a message one morning saying just this: 'Sick in chapel . . . mortifying. God will hate me forever'.

You name it, I know someone who's vommed in it. Or woken up in it, it would seem. I had a friend tell me how he'd once woken up wearing nothing but ski boots, with his arse in the air, after he'd fallen off the loo. Another who, while on tour with the army, had been given a few hours' R&R, only to wake up on a boat – despite the fact they were based 150 miles from water. I've got friends who have ended up at Paddington Station, where the trains are put to bed for the night, having slept past their stop, and ones who have woken up in Edinburgh thanks to similar circumstances. Doorsteps, gardens, pavements. We're as bad as each other, really. Well, some of us are worse than others – I actually have one friend who woke up on top of his garden shed using a dead squirrel as a blanket. Not only does he not know how he got there, he also has no idea where the squirrel came from and whether or not he was responsible for its death.

And all of that normally happens *after* you've caused us to fight with our friends, cry at inanimate objects, tell everyone that we love them, sing even though we can't, and dance all night. After we've said things we regret, snogged people we shouldn't have, cried, eaten disgusting food, started smoking again or phoned our exes. After we've spent money we don't have, lost everything we've ever owned, ruined a perfectly good pair of shoes and stayed up way too late. It happens after we've told strangers that we want to have their babies, woken up entire streets, forgotten how the fundamentals of using a key go, and completely disregarded all sense of personal safety believing that you have somehow made us car-proof.

But somehow, despite ALL this, I am grateful to you – because if it wasn't for you I wouldn't have some of my greatest memories. I wouldn't have spent a night in Dublin's most notorious gay club before going home and telling Alex I loved him for the first time. I wouldn't have watched my friend, dressed head to toe as a Power Ranger, fall backwards down an entire flight of stairs mid-sentence. (He's fine, I'm not a psychopath.) I wouldn't have repaired friendships I thought were unsalvageable. I would never have had my first kiss (well, hopefully I would at some point, but you know what I mean) and, ironically, considering the amnesia, I would have about 80 per cent less laugh-out-loud, clutch-your-stomach, treasure-forever memories if it hadn't been for you.

And, you know what, as I was drawing ideas for this chapter to a close, my friend Omey turned to me and said quietly, out of nowhere: 'I ate a candle when I was drunk once . . .' to which I replied, without even thinking, 'Oh, you think that's bad? I ate a sandwich full of cigarette butts for a dare a few years ago,' and nothing more was said about it.

And that, right there, is why I love you, dear Prosecco, so very, very much.

Em xx

Dear My Hair-straighteners

'But wait . . . did I leave my hair straighteners on?'

Every time, I turn around. Every time, I go home to check. Every time, I doubt myself. Every. Fucking. Time. You tell us that they turn themselves off after half an hour. Well, let's put it like this, shall we: if I'm paranoid enough to believe that I've left them on EVERY day, despite ALWAYS unplugging them at the wall, then I am NOT, repeat NOT, going to trust them to turn themselves off. Saying they do that on the box is not the reassurance you think it is. This is my HOUSE we're talking about. My house full of all my things and my beautiful dog and everything I love in this world. My house could go up in FLAMES if I've fucked this up and, just like that, everything I own, everything I love, would be GONE. Forever.

Are you SURE, Mr Straightener, that you'll definitely turn yourself off after half an hour? That absolutely nothing can go wrong? No. Because if I can't be sure that I turned you off, with my brain and my education and my extraordinary paranoia, then you, a piece of metal plugged into a wall, DEFINITELY won't. Straighteners need alarms. Really big, really loud, REALLY FUCKING

OBVIOUS alarms that go off once every thirty seconds. Please guys, for my sanity, consider this.

Em x
(someone who might not have turned her straighteners off)

Dear My Friends

A note to my friends, both past and present, good and bad. Thank you.

If my life on social media is anything to go by, there are loads of you; if my actual real life and calendar are to be believed, there is only a handful. To those of you that constitute the handful, thanks for being epic. To the rest of you, the aforementioned Facebook friends I met only once but bonded with immediately over a watered-down vodka Redbull and a mutual love of laughing gas, thank you also, for no other reason than some of you share mildly amusing pictures of cats dressed as people.

Between you, you have shaped me into the person I am today. Without you my life would be a much sadder place, although admittedly I probably wouldn't have been sick so much, my hair would never have had to suffer at the hands of one of you dying it orange, and I most likely wouldn't have had that first cigarette behind a tree in the school garden. On the plus side, though, it's thanks to you that I've done some great things. You encouraged me to travel the world, to start Pretty Normal Me, to get on a bike for the first time, to tell the love of my life how I felt about him, and ensure that my life has been more full of laughter than it has tears. Although you were to blame for some of the tears too. But I'll forgive you because you guys are my everything so, from the bottom of my heart, thank you.

Thank you for trusting me and, in turn, for making me want to be the best possible version of myself. Thank you for loving me and for needing me, and thank you for letting me love and need you. Thank you for making me happy.

Thank you to those of you who never gave up on me (although it would have been easier to) when I ditched the thought of university and moved to Dublin to basically be a glorified groupie. And thank you for being here when I returned, although many of you weren't and I can't blame you. Thank you to the ones who didn't give up on me when I declined invitations and ignored text messages. Thank you for waiting for me to get my head out of my arse and come back to you and thank you for having open arms when I did.

Thank you for holding back my hair, wiping my tears, for telling me I'm not fat, for making me laugh and for giving me the best memories a girl could ask for.

Thank you to the friend who agreed to dance to Britney's rendition of 'I Love Rock 'n' Roll' in front of an 800-strong audience of fellow pupils and discerning parents, in a knee-length pink skirt, neon vest and plastic pearls, even though neither of us could dance.

Thank you to all of you for the photoshoots we'd organise, and for not caring that it's actually incredibly weird to wear your only pair of high heels on a trampoline and pose, aged twelve. Thanks to this string of bright ideas, I now die of embarrassment and piss myself with laughter every time I see them.

Thank you to the friend who persuaded me that NO, it was NOT a good idea to try and organise a passport for a dog I found in a slum in Uganda so I could bring it home, but instead help me to find a home for it there. Thank you also for signing me up to a college to re-sit my A-Levels, even though you knew I didn't want to; it's nice to know you care.

Thank you to all the girls that took part in the weird 'thumbs up' or 'thumbs down' ritual at the parties we would go to in our early teens. With hindsight, though, this seems very odd: kissing a guy I hadn't even laid eyes on just because you, my friend, high on the idea of a snog and one too many Pro Plus pills, pointed her thumb in the direction of the ceiling.

Thank you to the friend who told me that mayonnaise was good for me; even though I now know it absolutely isn't, it's nice to know there's someone a little bit more deluded about food than me.

Thank you to the friend who pulled me through my first ever triathlon. Although it was hell on earth and I was so ready to quit, you got me through it, you made me enjoy it and, in turn, you helped me achieve something I will always remain incredibly proud of.

Thank you to all of the friends I've made through the charity Help for Heroes – those of you who have fought your way back from life-changing injuries to do incredible things have inspired me more than you will ever know. The fundraisers and patrons have made me realise what can be done when you set your mind to something, and the Band of Sisters (wives and girlfriends) have shown me the true meaning of love and sacrifice.

Thank you to my great friend who proofread this book for me and was honest in ways only you can be. My trust in you is unparalleled and you have shown me, over the last fifteen years of laughter and joy, what friendship is.

Thank you to my friend who built my website for me and still, weekly, sends me things you think I'll like. You have shown me that no matter how busy we get there should always be a big space in our lives for our friends. (I think you learned that from your incredible mother.)

Thank you to my friend who has had a trickier life than most but who, after raising her siblings as if they were her own, has shown to me what it really means to be strong for the ones you love. Your courage and bravery inspires me hugely.

Thank you to my boyfriend, my partner, the great love of my life, Alex. I genuinely don't know what I did to get so lucky, but if I've learned anything from being with you it's that we shouldn't question these things. We should live in the now and be happy with what we have and I am – I truly, truly am. I hope you know that you make my life complete. You have loved and supported me throughout the trickiest years of my life and, if it wasn't for you, I know I wouldn't be the person I am today. The idea of growing old used to scare me, of growing up and getting wrinkly and having children, but not anymore, because I know that in you I have a partner in crime and in life. I know that together we can achieve anything. You always say I'm daft when I thank you for loving me, but I'm not sure I am. I want you to know it and I need you to know it: I am very grateful for your love.

And to those of you who woke me from my drunken slumber at midnight on my eighteenth birthday to sing to me, thank you for not judging me as I promptly left the room to throw up everything you had told me was a good idea to drink that evening. In your own special way each of you has shaped me into the person I am today: the good, the bad and the really bloody ugly.

And even to those who have hurt me, I should probably thank you too. From the 'friend' who stole a photo from my Facebook profile and uploaded it with a creepy caption to *Reddit*; to the girl who only wanted me to sit next to her at school because I was Jeremy Clarkson's daughter, and to all of you social climbing nasties in between, thank you. You toughened me up, you gave me thicker skin and you taught me the value of forgiveness. Even though you are no longer in my life, I will never forget you, nor will I take for granted the fact that if it wasn't for you I'd still be the same naïve little being I always was, trusting every smile thrown my way. You taught me my very first 'how to survive having a vagina' lessons, and for those I will always be thankful.

And to the ones I have in turn hurt and let down: I'm sorry.

They say a true friendship can stand the test of time, but what they don't say of course is that both partners must at least try to remain loyal and good for that to be the case. In certain instances I have not been loyal and good and by doing that I took away any chance our friendship had. For that I am full of regret. I have not always been patient, I have not always been selfless, and I have not always been kind. I'm sorry that it took losing you for me to learn that but I know it now and I am truly so very sorry.

Please, forgive me?

The saying goes that 'good friends are like stars, you don't always see them, but you know they're always there', and it's true – each and every one of you is a star.

Because without you we are nothing. Without friends I would neither have anything nor be anything. Every day I'm inspired by you, empowered by you. The idea of loneliness scares me half to death; it has done since we learned 'Eleanor Rigby' in middle-school choir at my prep school. I am incredibly happy that the love of my life just so happens to be my best friend, but it doesn't mean and will never mean that I don't need all of you.

I am so grateful too that I'm able to have my best friend in my mum; it's a rare and precious thing, a friendship between mother and daughter, and something I cherish. Granted, I can't bat tattoo ideas to you, or ask you about your sex life but, as I'm discovering, there's a whole load more to friendship than gossip ... although that of course is great too and the foundations upon which many of my friendships were built.

I have a very cheesy mug in my cupboard that says 'friends are the family that you choose yourself', and although it makes me a bit queasy (I can't abide a soppy tagline in the kitchen), it's true. When I accepted you into my life, you became part of my family and I couldn't be happier. My life is full of the most fabulous and caring lunatics in the world and I wouldn't have it any other way.

There are many varieties of friends: fair-weather friends, friends you call when you need to get drunk, weekend friends, serious friends, friends that are more like siblings, friends of friends – whatever the occasion, a friend IS a friend and it's my duty not to let them down.

On our deathbeds our money will be of no use to us (unless of course we've used it to pay for a private room and lots of morphine), our houses, our cars, all irrelevant. What will be with us are our memories. And I don't want to have regret. I want to look back at the wonderful life I spent with some wonderful people, and smile. I want to be safe in the knowledge that I was a good friend and a good person.

Every day I work towards that moment. Every day I work to be the bestest friend I can be so that when we lie in our hospital pods of the future (beds will be old news by then) we will all have the best memories of the greatest people.

Seriously guys, thank you for the best twenty-odd years a girl could ask for. I might not say it enough, but I love you and I need you and I am so incredibly indebted to you.

You are all amazing.

Stay classy.

Em xxxx

Dear My 'Legal Stalkers' (a.k.a. My Facebook Friends)

Hi guys, just a quick one really and no big deal but I wanted to touch base with you because, if I'm honest, I've had about enough of quite a lot of your antics, so here's a list of things you do on Facebook that I've concluded are grounds to unfriend you:

Political rants

I KNOW you *have a voice*, that it's your God-given right to use it, and that you're totally entitled to make the most of your freedom of expression. I know that you really *care* and you really need for us to care about how much you care and, trust me, I know you think Theresa May is a blood-sucking, murdering bitch. But what you need to understand is this: I don't care what you think, none of us really do and, quite frankly, you sound like a twat. Have you heard of the saying 'opinions are like arseholes, everyone's got one and everyone's stinks'? TOTALLY appropriate here.

Hateful messages

All they make me do is hate you a little bit.

Inappropriate countdowns

This seems to be a tricky one to navigate for a lot of people, so I've broken it down for you: Appropriate – '100 days until Christmas' if and ONLY if accompanied by a fitting GIF, maybe of Buddy the Elf. Inappropriate – '432 days, 12 hours and 9 minutes until I buy the shoes for my wedding'. All that makes me do is realise that for the next 432 days, 12 hours and 9 minutes you are going to be the most annoying thing since the Crazy Frog. I'm sorry, but most of your friends *really* don't care.

Passive-aggressive confessions

By this I of course mean posts such as: 'now I know who my true friends are'. We see right through that and know full well that the translation is: THE REST OF YOU ARE ALL SHIT. ASK ME HOW I AM IMMEDIATELY.

The 'IV drip selfie' with NO other explanation

Are you OK? Damn it. You got what you wanted, you drew me in and now I'm sitting here worrying that you might have Ebola. But you OBVIOUSLY don't have Ebola, do you? Please imagine my frustration when I went out of my way to ask all of our mutual friends what's going on only to find out that you have an ingrowing toenail.

'Here's my new house, car AND Tiffany necklace, isn't my BF the best?'

Yes, he is. My boyfriend bought me a carrot peeler about a month ago but you didn't see me bragging about that, did you? Nope, because I'm not a dick.

Ten photos of your baby doing the same thing in EVERY picture

Yes, it's cute. It's a baby, so of course it is. And yes, it's a miracle that you squished that out of a vagina. But ten photos of him sucking on gravel? I don't care.

Relentless motivational memes to get you through a mysterious 'tough time'

What is this tough time? Who's dead? Is it acceptable to 'like' this? Who is this message really meant for? Is it meant for me? STOP SPEAKING IN RIDDLES WOMAN AND TELL ME WHAT THE BLOODY HELL IS GOING ON.

Look at all the stamps in my passport and all of the amazing holidays I go on

'My job is just the best; they pay me to go the Bahamas like every other weekend!' SHUT UP. Go and enjoy your holiday like a normal person.

The 'I-just-woke-up-like-this' selfie that has clearly been planned about twelve years in advance

You didn't just wake up like that; you can't fool me. Take it over to Instagram bbz. That's what it's there for. #nofilter

Your Strava updates

Oh, you ran 5.4 km this morning, did you? Great. Good for you. I just spent forty minutes mustering the strength to walk to the fridge, so who's the real winner here, eh?

The 'most of my friends won't share this' guilt trip

Don't make me feel like a prick PLEASE. I don't need this validation and nor do you. I'm not going to copy and paste this, it won't fix the world and I won't get eaten by a bear if I don't, nor will my family be struck down by lightning. This was invented by someone who loves their CAPLOCKS and not their splelchekc. You're better than that.

★ ★ ★

I will of course make exceptions to these rules; nobody's perfect, sometimes we can't help ourselves and I'm not a total Grinch, but these exceptions are few and far between. Generally speaking, if you are guilty of two or more of these, you're going to have to go – for my sanity. I can't take it.

And just because I ought to prove that I'm not a totally miserable cow when it comes to online friendships, here are the things I love to see:

- Wedding photos. (The lighting is usually nice.)
- Family photos. (Reminds me that we are capable of interacting in real life.)
- Videos of people falling over. (I have a pathological problem and live for this.)
- Photos of cats in clothes. (*Cats in clothes*, guys . . .)
- The videos of the dogs eating like humans. (*Dogs eating like humans*, guys . . .)
- Graduation photos. (Makes me proud.)
- Interesting articles. (Obvious.)
- Great drunk photos from a night out. (They're usually funny.)

- Engagement ring photos. (I'm happy for you.)
- Ultrasounds. (That's INSANE there is a baby in your tummy.)
- 'I got promoted' posts. (You've worked hard and that's great.)
- Proud parent moments. (They melt my heart.)
- Memes that GENUINELY make me laugh or nod. (I like laughing and nodding.)
- Basically anything that shows you actually DO some interesting stuff with your life.

See you on your birthday, I guess, when Facebook reminds me. Despite all of this, I do love you guys,

Em xx

Dear My Body

FAO: My body hair, my stomach rolls and every part of me that has ever been sunburnt

You totally blow my mind; you know that, right? You're a medical marvel. The fact that my six-foot-two brother, for example, LIVED in the stomach of my five-foot-one mother as she grew him. Or that while I'm just minding my own business, cracking on with life, my heart is pumping blood around my body. Or even that when I'm asleep and can control nothing, I somehow keep on breathing in and out. All these little things that I take for granted. Sometimes I'll accidentally feel my own pulse and freak the fuck out at the madness of it all. YOU'RE SO CLEVER.

I don't say it enough, but you are amazing, you really are. You also don't deserve half of what I put you through, so I need to say this: I'm sorry for jabbing you so full of holes. I'm sorry I love coffee and Jägerbombs so much. I'm sorry for the time I shoved my hand into an electric whisk just to see what would happen. I'm sorry for filling you with tar on a daily basis. I'm sorry that processed crap tastes so good and that I'm so rubbish at saying no to any of it. I'm sorry for squishing you into jeans every day. I'm sorry for starving you pre-holidays. I'm sorry for lathering you up in oil and effectively cooking you once we're on said holidays. I'm sorry for suffocating my pores with foundation every day. I'm sorry for singeing my hair so regularly. I'm sorry for relentlessly ripping the rest of my hair out of my skin. I'm sorry for strapping enormous plastic sticks to my feet and throwing myself down a mountain once a year. I'm sorry in advance for my plans to use you as an oven for a little human. I'm sorry that I insist on filling you so full of alcohol that it prevents my wonderful legs from working. I'm sorry that I spent so many years in shoes that were too small or too high. I'm sorry that I don't moisturise enough or sleep for very long. I'm sorry that I chose for us to live in a city where the air is totally filthy. I'm sorry I don't wear my glasses all the time even though I should. I'm sorry for not taking care of you nearly as well as I ought.

As I write it all down I see there is plenty of room for improvement and so, as of now, I do pledge to do what I can to make that right. Or maybe not *right* but better. I will try to make it better, OK? Now, seeing as you have no choice but to forgive me, and since I intend (well, hope) to stick around for a fair few years yet, I think I also ought to say thank you a few million times as well. I need to say thank you, for everything.

For my ability to see, to breathe, to walk, to think and to taste, thank you thank you thank you. Every morning I am able to open my eyes, yawn and stretch, before putting my feet on the floor and using my legs to stand up. Every day I am able to walk down the stairs to the fridge, where I can eat food – nice food that I like AND that keeps me alive. I am able to pack a bag and leave the house and go places. ANY places. Every day I see amazing things, and DO amazing things, and every day I take these things for granted.

I take you for granted every single day, not because I mean to but because I forget. I forget that other people aren't as lucky as me, that they can't do the things I can simply because their bodies won't permit it. I don't take into consideration enough that some people have bad knees and bad backs; that some people have lost limbs or are confined to chairs. Nor do I think enough about those whose minds slip away from them and they lose the ability to remember things, or to talk. Every day I take for granted the fact that I am incredibly lucky; so really, thank you.

I get so caught up in squeezing you and judging you and hating you that I forget to appreciate all the good stuff. Given half the chance, I'm ready to criticise you to anyone who'll listen. I tell them that my back aches, that my stomach is too fat, that I have dry hair, that I'm really spotty, that I'm too short. I say that my nails don't grow fast enough or that my skin is really dry. I complain that my boobs are too flat or my teeth are not straight. I complain about you all the time and, because my incredibly well-designed ears are so close to my mouth, you have to hear it every day. I don't know how that must feel. Depressing? Probably. Boring? Maybe. Annoying? Definitely.

I'm sorry I'm so horrible about you. I'm sorry that in the past I haven't loved you. But I realise now: so what we have stomach rolls? So what we get spots? Really, that is a small price to pay for all the amazing stuff we do together, isn't it? Together we have driven across Africa, cycled all the way across Europe, done a triathlon, written a book, completed fifteen years of education, gone up all 193 stairs at Covent Garden tube station without stopping for a break, climbed the Great Wall of China, fallen in love with someone. We've done SO much together. Everything I am is you, and together we are pretty frickin' great.

As a thank you for all of the hard work you do, I pledge to start rewarding you. We will take more baths, stop smoking (one day), eat less crap, do exercise that doesn't nearly kill us or damage our joints, take vitamins, sleep more and moisturise. God, I really want to start moisturising. We will start putting treatment in our hair and meditating. We'll wear bras that fit properly and I will ensure that every so often I fill you up with the cleanest, healthiest air I can find. I will be a better grown-up and take better care of you, I promise. And in return? All I ask is that you keep doing what you're doing. Keep being great.

I'm sorry I spent so long hating you. I'm sorry that some days I still do. You don't deserve that; you are amazing and I would do well to remember that. How about this: next time I go to squeeze a roll of fat somewhere with the intention of complaining, give me a cold. Or failing that, remove a limb. Start with the fingers. Let's see how well I can light a fag without them. I'll soon realise how good I had it.

I don't say it enough, but I love you.

Thank you.

Em xxxx

Dear The Bottomless Pit That Is My Handbag

I am a handbag girl. I believe you are just the most beautiful things in the world, that you are an investment, that you are things of great work and craftsmanship, that you are things to be admired and adored. I look at myself in the mirror when I'm holding you and think, Good God, that girl has class. I stroke your soft leather exterior. I sometimes go as far as to smell you. I breathe you in and feel wonderful as I do it. I slowly go to unzip you, shifting the position at which you're sitting on my shoulder to do it, and I gently slip my hand in . . . it is here that I find hell on earth.

My wallet, my notebook, my diary, my phone, my portable charger, my car keys, my house keys, my perfume, my laptop. My laptop charger, my card reader, a pen. Another pen, and then another pen. A hair tie, a dog lead, a lipstick. Another pen. A receipt for a round of tequilas, a boarding pass from 2002, a packet of dog treats. A packet of Neurofen, a set of keys to a house I moved out of three years ago, a hairclip. A full packet of cigarettes. Three empty packets of cigarettes, no lighter. Another pen. A packet of dried mango, a pair of old socks, a furry Strepsil stuck to an old train ticket. A pair of headphones (knotted to shit), one earring, some poo bags. A boarding pass from 2006, another pen. Some hand cream, some foot cream, some lip balm. A teabag, a pamphlet, a receipt for another round of tequilas. An eyeliner, a ring, a small wooden stick that at one point smelt of perfume. Some 2p coins, a 10p coin, a collection of coins from countries I have never been to in my life. Another pen. The other earring. A stick of concealer, something that looks like it could be dried nail varnish, a pair of glasses, the television remote control and a, YAY, oh no, wait, a broken lighter. A tampon, an empty packet of crisps, some contact lens fluid, some sand, half a piece of chewing gum, a tape measure, a business card, a boarding pass from 2012. Nine kirby grips, a hand mirror and another fucking pen.

People laughed at Mary Poppins – they thought she was mad for carrying around her life in her bag, but I never did. In fact, not only do I understand her, I admire the girl. Because I know what life is like lugging around all the shit that I do on a daily basis, and if she's got the strength to literally manage the kitchen sink I tip my hat to her, I really do.

Thanks for everything,

Em xx

Dear The Owners Of A Resting Bitch Face (Of Which I Am One)

cc Anyone who lives in London

Girls, it saddens me to say this but we need a chat. I think our RBFs (resting bitch faces) might, as it turns out, be slightly more of an issue than any of us had first thought. Although useful in crowded streets and on busy trains, and although they are something totally out of our control, the time has come for the RBF to go. I speak to you as the owner of one, so I know, as I write this, that I'm asking a lot. I'm pretty much asking you to get a new face, and I know I sound ridiculous but there is logic behind this one, I promise you.

Let me tell you why. As you know, our condition – our resting bitch face – means that we permanently look pissed off or sad or mean. I don't know the science of it exactly, why nature made us this way, but I know a lot of us are affected by it, that there are many variants on the condition – even if the result is the same – and that, as of now, there is no known cure. Some of our mouths naturally curve downwards at the sides, some of our eyebrows fight to be together through the medium of frowning, and some

of us lose any warmth in our eyes when we stop focusing
on something specific. Jaws lock, frown lines appear, smiles
seem out of the question.

We could have had the best news in the world from our
doctor, who might have JUST told us that we DON'T have
an STD after all, and we would still look, as my mother
would say, like a slapped arse. Which would be fine, it's our
face after all, except for the fact that while on the way home
from the doctors, arse face in all its glory, the chances are we
are going to cross paths with someone who perhaps doesn't
share the affliction; a person with a normal face, who might
have had a bad day and who might just have appreciated
some positive affirmation in the shape of a smile – or at
least a hint of one – from a passer-by. But instead this poor
creature, upon bumping into us, is met with the full force
of an RBF, which is, quite frankly, terrifying. In fact, I
think it's having some fairly catastrophic implications on the
confidence of women everywhere and, for that reason and
that reason alone, I think we need to work on this.

Underneath my RBF, in case you didn't know already,
I'm a bit of a softy. I wouldn't be surprised if you were too.
In fact, I'm not sure there's an RBF owner alive who hasn't,
at some point in their lives, had a complete and utter crisis
of confidence and needed nothing more than a hug and a
biscuit and the promise that everything is going to get better
in a bit. So it won't have been a surprise to you when I made
the link between our slapped-arse faces and other women's
insecurities, and nor will it be a surprise to you when I admit
that, because of our kind, I am regularly left halfway down

a street riddled with insecurity, usually thanks to one look from one girl that has made me want nothing more than to run to my bed as fast as I can, crawl under my duvet and basically never do anything again. Because whether we'll admit it or not, most of us know that one wrong look from another woman is enough to shatter into a million pieces what little confidence we had mustered that day. (Of course this isn't an everyday occurrence, or our kind would have ensured that nothing ever got done. But it is a thing, and it's something we've gotta talk about.)

Now really, an RBF shouldn't be that big a deal to me; I live in London, after all, which is THE capital of the RBF. We Londoners are taught early on that we mustn't smile at each other, that it's weird and out of place, quite unnecessary and kind of suspicious. But guys, I'm going to go against everything I've spent years believing to be true and say it might not be. Let me explain. Here is the internal monologue that happens in my head when I pass another woman with an RBF:

'Hey, what does she want? Kind of nasty. Actually wait, that was REALLY nasty. Like, more than nasty. That literally penetrated my soul. I felt it; it went right through me. What warranted that, do you think? It's the skirt, isn't it? OH GOD. I fucking knew it. WHAT WAS I THINKING? This is the shortest skirt in all the land. Kinda cute when you're nine-foot tall with legs like those skinny little trees you see planted at ceremonies. NOT when they look like the 4,000-year-old tree trunks that they're doing documentaries on, on BBC2. Fucking thunder-thighs.

WHY DID I THINK THIS WAS A GOOD IDEA? She smelt the cellulite, didn't she? That's why her nose went into that weird crinkle. It's SO short I wanna die, let me see if I can pull it down ... NOPE. Fuck. I bet she thinks I'm a massive slag, judging the LIFE out of me right now. In what world would someone like that be my friend? Seriously, what chance do I stand at anything if I can't even get dressed right? Look at the state of me. I am a mess. SO permanently sloppy, why can't I ever just look the bloody part? I am NEVER going to make something of my life; I'll never have it all together like she does. HOW am I supposed to go into work now? Have I got time to go home and get changed? No, of course I haven't, and even if I did, what the tits would I wear? Did you SEE what she had on? She looked savage. I don't own anything remotely like that. I bet she smells SO good. The judgey ones always do. I bet I don't. Oh lord, maybe she smelt me. Not the cellulite, ME! What if I smell?! Holy moly, I can't even deal. I am genuinely revolting. How am I meant to face the world now? Like, get on with life as if NOTHING EVER HAPPENED? I can't, I just can't. No one will ever love me. I am totally unemployable. I hate the world. I just need to be back in bed right now. I'm going to die alone. Always alone, worth nothing. NOTHING.'

Now take a look at the internal monologue that happens when I pass a woman on the street who smiles at me:

'Wait, did that beautiful woman just smile at me? Amazing. That was adorable. Do I know her? She doesn't look familiar ... no, I don't think I do. Confusing. Did she just smile because she's a nice person, if so: AHMAZING.

That was so NICE. I'll smile back, that seems like the right thing to do. Yup, it's working, we're smiling at each other, this is so easy and adorable. What a nice little moment that was. I bet we'd be great friends. What a treat. This is a good day . . .

  ＊＊Strolls into the imaginary sunset＊＊

  I don't know about you, but I know which spiral I would like to send someone into. You see, we totally take for granted the power our faces hold. I hate to admit it – hell, I hate it in general – but I am famed for my flexible face, and not always for the right reasons. My right eyebrow has a nasty habit of heading towards the heavens when I'm confused or unimpressed, and my family have mastered their impersonation of my withering stare – the one I find hard to stop when something has angered me. It actually breaks my heart to see this because I hate the idea of being 'known' for something so horrid. Not least because I spend a lot of time trying so hard to be *nice,* and to know that I don't *look* it is actually kind of hurtful.

  'OK, Em, but HOW am I supposed to barge through the crowds on Oxford Street with any authority if I don't have my RBF on?!' Guys, I hear ya. Sometimes an RBF is the most powerful tool in your arsenal. There are times when, particularly as a woman, the RBF or an authoritative face – to those out there who don't own one would naturally call it – is required. (Although that does make me a bit sad to say.) When a man is leaning out of his car window to heckle you, when you are not being taken seriously in the office, or when someone thinks it's funny to say that women are only good for making sandwiches and giving blowjobs, it does have its uses, don't get me wrong. Nothing tells an ignorant little pig man to shut up like the icy glare of someone whose face actually sits like that. But when they're used on another woman, albeit accidentally, the results can be catastrophic and that is something we need to bear in mind.

My whole *thing* – the whole point of me and the blog and this book and everything I stand for – is based on the fact that women don't do enough to support one another. It's one of my biggest concerns and really has everything to do with why I started Pretty Normal Me. Bitchiness in schools happens between girls; decisions made in the fashion industry that see size zero models hired and clothes not going bigger than a size 16 are made by women, and the reason I still can't bring myself to go to a yoga class and better myself is because of the hordes of women ready to judge the life out of me for farting mid-downward dog.

It doesn't take a genius to see it; we are inherently competitive and often can't help ourselves from being judgemental. It often surprises me when I hear women describing other women as 'slags', to hear them commenting on the length of another woman's skirt, or questioning whether or not her behaviour is 'ladylike'. I am equally saddened to hear about bitchy behaviour between women in the workplace because *surely* we should be building each other up. Alas, that doesn't happen as much as it should and I'm pretty sure that a lot of it starts with a look – or more specifically with *our* look, the RBF look.

Because the assumption goes, for me at least, something like this: 'Ooh, a new woman, she probably hates me. She's got better legs and is therefore much more impressive than me in every single way.' That's just the way my brain works. It's weird, I grant you, but I don't think it's unusual and so, here I am, ready to call time on it. Actually, begging us all to call time on it.

Did you know that it takes twenty-six muscles to smile, whereas it takes sixty-two to frown? Which basically means that by being permanently grumpy we are actually using WAY more effort than we would if we could whip our friendly faces out. Did you also know that smiling is contagious? And that when we force ourselves to do it, it ACTUALLY makes us feel better? Did you know that smiling was your first facial expression? Or that it can reduce blood pressure and that employers are more likely to hire a smiley person? It's the universal sign for happiness; it's actually pretty flipping wonderful in general. Why *wouldn't* we want that? We'd be mad not to. Smiling is actually really, really nice. YAY for smiling. Let's all smile.

Guys, I KNOW your RBF served you well when you were at school and you needed to terrorise the younger years into fearing and respecting you. I know it's useful AF in the garage when the guy changing your tyre adopts a voice implying that the concept of the wheel might be slightly beyond your understanding, and I know you basically NEED it when your mum asks you for the billionth time to show you how to upload a photo on the 'Face Page'. But you don't need it on the streets anymore.

Nothing bad will happen: you won't lose all the respect you worked so hard to build, people won't start taking advantage of you left, right and centre, and you won't get arrested. What might happen instead could be any of the following:

- You will make someone's bus journey
- You will make someone's morning
- You will make someone's day
- You will make someone's week

Maybe the person you next smile at hasn't been smiled at in AGES. Maybe their cat just died. Maybe they're wearing green lipstick for the first time and they're really, really nervous about it. Maybe, just maybe, they really need this right now.

If you can't face saying goodbye to your *internal* RBF then so be it but, whatever you do, keep the public one under wraps from now on.

Smile, please. It really is great.

Love y'all.

Em xxxx

Dear Body Hair

cc Wax strips, epilators and that horrendously smelly hair-removal cream

Hello! First things first, I need to tell you that I am so, so sorry. I've literally been the worst. I have treated you appallingly and I cannot say I'm sorry enough times. It's not you. It's definitely me. You never did anything wrong. On the contrary, all you ever tried to do was keep me warm, as nature intended, and I have repaid you by either slicing you in half or ripping you out. I don't know what to say for myself. It's a disgrace. I am really sorry.

I don't want to make a whole ton of excuses for myself here, because after what I've done I'm really not entitled to, BUT I just need to quickly say . . . society made me do it. (Hot potato now in their hands.) You see, where you, body hair, is concerned, we've got all these rules that we need to adhere to; all this pressure on us to be as smooth as a baby's arse, and this fear that, God-forbid, if a man should find a hair on you . . . well, that's game over. It's time to go to the pet rescue centre, adopt as many cats as they'll allow, stock up on white wine and fags and brace yourself for a life of spinsterdom. We really have been taught to believe that you aren't good, and I am ashamed to say that you have been my sacrifice in my bid to 'get it right'.

Despite the fact that the feminist movement has for a long time been led by women brave enough to banish the razor and embrace the fur, the idea of going *au naturel* is still something the world is yet to accept as appropriate. In fact, sadly, before starting this book I asked a whole collection of people, both men and women, to tell me the first word that popped into their head when they thought of a 'feminist' and 'hairy' was one of the most popular (followed closely by 'bossy', 'aggressive', 'militant' and 'lonely' (**✱✱** thwacks head against wall repeatedly**✱✱**). Although the two aren't necessarily mutually exclusive, the negative connotations surrounding both are still a monster of an issue and, as a result, having body hair is just not considered attractive. It's seen as unhygienic and, it would seem, by growing it out you are by definition a raging, left-wing, man-hating feminist, which *definitely* isn't what the youth of today want to aspire to **✱✱** thwacks again**✱✱**. That is what my brutality is about; I am part of the youth of today. It's not an excuse but I hope that it acts as a bit of an explanation.

And yet I'm a firm believer that where one's bush is concerned a lot of men don't *really* care. Although they think they know what they want – having wasted their adolescence goggling at bald women bending every which way trying to take three dicks at once and pretending to enjoy it – there are a couple of fundamental reasons that, in my opinion, prevent them from caring:

- Most of them are so bloomin' grateful to have a naked woman in front of them, or to have at least gained access to the treasure chest they spend their lives searching for, that they couldn't give two flying fucks what it looked like. They are not, I repeat NOT going to give up the opportunity of getting their dick wet (sorry, I've been watching some really sexist, trashy TV of late) just because you haven't had time to 'sort yourself out'. They might tell their mates that they wouldn't go near a 'furry beaver' with a bargepole, but they're lying.

  I reckon most of them would still have a pop if it could talk, made the occasional joke and sounded like Alan Carr.

- They love you, or should at least respect you enough to know and appreciate that no one really has the time or the money to spend once a month with a stranger staring at their pussy while making polite conversation, covering them in hot wax and putting them through absolute hell. They also know that, much like everything else in this life, it's what on the inside that counts. They would not refuse to take a woman out to dinner because they didn't like the jacket she was wearing. I think it's fundamentally the same story with her vagina.

But of course, many of us are not willing to risk finding this out for ourselves. Most of us are scared that should a man venture down there and find out what a 'REAL

WOMAN LOOKS LIKE' he will do a full 180 and run out leaving nothing but a cloud of dust in his wake. Worse still, we worry that he won't stop running until he gets to the dwelling in which ALL THE MEN reside and will tell them the ugly truth about us. He will expose us for the revolting creatures we are and that'll be that, we'll be on the way to the pet rescue centre before the dust settles.

No matter how liberal we *think* we are, no matter how far we *think* we have come, there are still countless women spending countless hours removing countless hairs proving that this pressure is as big, if not bigger, than it has ever been before and is something we just have to conform to. You have to see the pressure we're under. I don't know what you did to piss off the Society Gods SO badly but whatever it was they're not in a rush to forgive you. As a result, we really don't have any choice but to banish you. I wish there was another way but I don't think there is. I hope you understand.

NB. To those of you now screeching at the page about that time in the early noughties when Julia Roberts flipped the bird to the haters in the most epic way by walking down the red carpet with a small gerbil under each arm . . . I hear ya. And although this was badass and great, and a step in the right direction, have we let her forget it? Have we fuck. The world just isn't *ready* for armpit hair right now **I'm still thwacking**.

My mum always said to me, 'Never remove any body hair without speaking to me first,' which I think is actually pretty sound advice, but annoyingly I only seem to remember hearing that for the first time after I'd mutilated my eyebrows beyond recognition and taken away their chance at a long, happy, natural life. (I'M SORRY! Why are you still punishing me for this? Grow back . . . *pleeeeease!*) Or I must have thought I just knew better but, either way, I'd do an awful lot to turn back the clock on that one. And that was just the start of it because, unfortunately, it's not simply a question of to shave or not to shave. There are, I now know, a whole ton of options for us to damage and remove you and lots of scope for fucking it up.

I clearly remember the first time I shaved my legs. I have no recollection of the first go under my arms, or even of my eyebrows, but the legs I remember well: I had somehow acquired a six-pack of tiny yellow disposable razors which, for some reason, I was hiding in my desk in my room. (I suppose I'd heard Mum's warnings after all and had chosen to ignore them.) I must have been about twelve and had absolutely no idea what I was doing, so I did what I thought seemed right. I sat myself down on my bedroom floor, pulled down my trousers to expose dry skin and blonde leg hair and got to work. No water, no cream, no soap. It was like Sweeney Todd. Not only did I look like a raw chicken, I was bleeding from everywhere connected to a bone. Surely this couldn't be what all the fuss was about? I then remember the overwhelming sense of shame that came over me afterwards: I couldn't look anyone in the eye, my cheeks flushed red whenever anybody asked me a question and I wore nothing but tights until it grew back, for fear of what my mum would say if she noticed. (That was probably the one and only time I thanked you for growing back so fast!) I don't remember trying again after that. I suppose I must have kept going because for the life of me I can't remember a time when my legs weren't either really stubbly or smooth as silk.

I also remember the first time I went for a wax – ahem – down there. Holy shit tits. WHY? I was fifteen and about to head to Glastonbury and I genuinely don't know why I did it; it certainly wasn't 'for' anyone, if you catch my drift. (Would it hurt your feelings less if I'd said someone made me do it and that I wasn't acting of my own volition?) I suppose I just went because my friends were doing it, I thought it was the 'done' thing and, if I'm honest, it made me feel pretty bloody grown up. And in fairness, after the initial pain subsided and I stopped looking like the last turkey in the shop and was able to walk properly again, I actually kind of liked it. I DID feel grown up and, in the week before you grew back in the most irritating way, I was pleased as punch with my bald bits.

But what surprises me about all this looking back on it was how young I was when it all started. How my friends and I, without having it properly explained to us, somehow just knew what needed to be done, and that my mum was so weirdly accepting of it, actually encouraging it. I'm making her sound like some kind of pushy beauty pageant 'mom', but I don't mean it like that; it's just so strange to think that this is so accepted.

You have a daughter, so ergo one day you'll buy her an epilator and tell her to use it because it's '*Soooo* much better than shaving, and one day you'll never look back . . . the pain is WORTH IT!'

'But WHY, Mum? Why do I have to be in pain?'

'I don't know, dear, it's just part of being a woman.'

Ah, that old chestnut. Being a woman. Being a FUCKING woman. See, this issue is more deep-rooted (pardon the pun) than perhaps you'd first thought. It's more than a question of my preferring plucked eyebrows. This is gender equality shit right here. Look what you're involved with; just one of the many inequalities that comes with BEING A WOMAN.

I just *love* the choices that we get to make. I love the choice that I get to make between wearing high heels and not looking smart enough in my office. I love the choice between putting make-up on and having everyone speculating behind my back that I might have let myself go. I love the choice between sending a very revealing photo of myself to a man and being frigid. The choices we get to make on a daily basis to prevent us getting judged and feeling different are just FAB, aren't they?

The kind of choices I like to make are generally between burgers and pizzas, or between the beach and the pool, not rip out all of your body hair or risk dying alone. But here we are. You give a fifteen-year-old girl that ultimatum and you can be fairly sure what she'll go for. Hell, you give a forty-year-old woman the same one and her answer wouldn't differ. We do what we think the world wants us to. Hell, we do what the world DOES want us to.

Please pass this on to all the other body hair out there too; relay them this paragraph. Make them see that no matter how hard they *think* life is as someone's pube, it could be worse . . . at least they are not a woman.

Luckily with age comes wisdom, and many of us have learned that, really, it is our body and it would take a brave man to comment on the state of our bush. I've been in my relationship for over four years, and if I can't be arsed to get a wax or I decide to go straight from October to March without shaving my legs, Alex has very little choice but to like it or lump it. But for younger girls? Girls at school? What huge fucking pressure.

'Why did I have my first wax? All it took was for one girl to say, "Oh, boys hate public hair," and that was it, we all started to do it. I don't even know how she knew this; she must have read it somewhere, I guess . . .'

This was the observation of one of my friends, now twenty-four, about the first time she stripped her private parts of its coat, aged fourteen.

But what I want to know is where the HELL did this girl, that friend of a friend, read that comment? *Cosmo*? *Glamour*? *Elle*? *Heat*? Did you have a falling out with an editor or something? Must have done, 'cos articles like that aren't appearing in *GQ*, I'll tell you that for nothing. She read this in a magazine written for women, by women, I'll bet you all my money. And this is a fear being instilled in us way, way too young.

That same friend has now thankfully seen sense. She went on to tell me that: 'I can understand why they don't want to deal with a 1970s bush where they have to fight their way, explorer-style, to the clit, but it's my vagina . . .'

But where was that quote when I was thirteen? Where were the women telling me that? Where were the men standing up and saying, 'You know what, girls? It's your vagina, and no, I don't LOVE it, much like you probably don't appreciate my hairy ballsac, but it's bloody expensive, I'm not willing to pay for it, and if you're really only doing it for my benefit, then worry not. I'll let you into a secret . . . we just don't care *that* much.'

Why did no one tell me that by keeping you I could still grow up to be anything I wanted to be?

So there you go. There is my explanation, my excuse – call it what you want. I am sorry, truly I am. I don't treat you right. Having said that, and actually meant it, I also ought to say that despite my apology and my somewhat random desire to keep you in protest, I don't actually like you that much. Maybe if things were different I would but, right now, I don't. You are a faff, you are an inconvenience, and I do actually think my life would be a helluva lot easier if you weren't in it. If I had the money – and wasn't slightly concerned it might turn me into a radioactive superhuman – then I would probably have had you all lasered off by now, because society told me that's what I should do.

Not in so many words, but in the same way I feel like I need to wear high heels to a black-tie function, that I don't look smart without make-up, that if I'm going for a job interview I need to take my nose-ring out, that I shouldn't talk about pooing in front of boys, that this summer I need

to be beach body ready. Sometimes it's easier to just roll
over and take it than constantly fight the good fight. I'm
not proud of myself for saying that. It's not right but, where
you're concerned, you've got to understand that.

So although I don't like you I do apologise because, under
different circumstances, I would really like to love you. And
I hope against hope that one day soon there'll be other little
Em Clarksons wandering around, bushes poking out of the
tops of their trousers, gerbils planning the great escape from
underneath their arms and wool on their legs and being
absolutely fine about it. I'm sorry that society has made us
hate you, I'm sorry that it's put you out of business, and I'm
sorry that I'm adhering to this wanky pressure.

Hopefully I'll see you around one day soon.

All my love,

Em xx

Dear Make-up

I don't think we need much of an introduction, do we? I mean, you know me so well. You literally spend so much of your time sitting on my face (thanks for that) and hiding all my spots from the world (massive, massive thanks for that).

I'm writing to you because I am beyond confused and I need you to clear up a whole ton of stuff for me. Everywhere I look, there you are, an unspoken law when it comes to a woman's life – on the face of every woman who has ever felt a spot coming on, in the handbag of the old woman next to me on the bus and on the mind of every young girl who dreams of the day she won't need to pad her bra anymore.

You are this amazing gift we've been given to mask our flaws, accentuate the assets we're proud of and the opportunity to change our identity. For that, thank you; really and truly, thank you.

But with the same hand that you give us all of these amazing opportunities and confidence, you seem to be handing out nothing but insecurity. As empowering as you are, when it boils down to it, by giving us the tools to make our faces look 'better', you are sort of implying there was something wrong with them in the first place. Of course, this isn't really your fault, but the very nature of your existence does make me question the sanity of female kind, that we find ourselves going to such extreme lengths to 'better' ourselves.

Every day, through using you, the average woman is using 168 chemicals on her body; most of us spend time literally painting our faces, colouring in our lips and drawing around our eyes like children with their homework. We're late to things because of the application time, we are less able to enjoy ourselves without you on, and you've been known to ruin many a pool party in your time. And although I know my make-up skills are beyond efficient, I have been known to spend well over an hour 'redecorating' when really I could have been out enjoying my life.

And although this isn't your fault, I have to say it is a little bit annoying that in this day and age women are made to feel they are 'expected' to wear you. This is a statement that will be vehemently denied by a few women I know, but let's face it, we just are. If a woman showed up to a job interview without you on, you can almost guarantee that her abilities would be called into question. If a girl goes to a party without you on, she must be ill. And if one day a girl just stopped wearing you all together, well, oh, my gosh, isn't she just the BRAVEST? (Just for the record, working in bomb disposal is BRAVE. Going without make-up? Don't even get me started . . .)

But contrary to popular belief, or at least the beliefs of parents of 'kids these days', make-up is not new and little girls wanting to wear it to school is not new. In fact, our quest for self-improvement is a concept as old as time, and it's not your fault; you're just a by-product of it. You are an invention we came up with to make ourselves look and feel better, and so although I understand people's need to air their frustrations about your existence in the first place, I think it's high time my twenty-first-century sisters (and brothers) took the time to appreciate how good we have it.

Your existence came about as a result of Roman women using belladonna drops to make their pupils look larger and sexier, even though those drops were actually poison. They were also said to have whitened their teeth by gurgling urine. In the Elizabethan era, women would use arsenic and lead in a bid to keep them as pale as possible, they would use coal tar as mascara, which caused many of them to go blind, and, in medieval times, they would even use leeches, yes LEECHES, to maintain a milky complexion. They were SO desperate to be 'beautiful' that they would literally have the blood sucked out of themselves.

But us 2017 gals? We don't appreciate how badly we want you, because you have always been here for us. And to those people who think that perhaps if you hadn't been invented the world would be a much nicer place (no offence), tell them they're wrong. Because even if you didn't exist right now it would only be a matter of time before some other insecure little girl stuck her head into the fireplace to make her eyelashes look longer. Your not being here is not a realistic notion, so don't worry, your job is safe.

While you do admittedly open the door for bullying, judgement and insecurity, short of hopping back 6,000 years and telling the pioneers of self-improvement that, 'One day, many thousands of years from now, there will be a little girl called Emily Clarkson feeling left out because all her friends are wearing make-up to school while she doesn't own any', and that it is, 'All your fault for making her feel she needed to change herself in the first place, SO STEP AWAY FROM THE LEECHES ...' there's just not much we can do about it, is there? Because if it hadn't been you it would have been something else.

So I get it, you're here to stay and there's nothing we can do about that. But what I really want to know is WHY? Why is it that Americans are now spending more on you than on education? Why is it that you are now the biggest industry in the world? And why is it that one in three women refuses to leave the house without you on? Because that's the bit that worries me.

Since hearing this statistic I've been trying to work out our relationship. Would I refuse to go out without you on? No. Because I'm fundamentally a lazy person and the idea of putting it on and taking it off again for a run to the shops is too much for me. But am I comfortable completely barefaced out and about? No, not really.

If Alex were to come home from work and see me covered in make-up, he would more readily assume I'd got bored in front of the mirror than that I was conducting a secret affair, because he knows that, generally speaking, I love wearing make-up for me and not for other people. Any man that isn't interested in a make-up-free me is not a man worth knowing as far as I'm concerned, and he knows that.

But these days it's quite rare for me to do anything

without at least a little bit of concealer on. Because even though the rest of the world doesn't seem to notice when I have a spot – or so they say – I do, and it has recently really started to ruin my life. (Yes, I am a colossal drama queen.)

There is of course the age-old question, who do we wear make-up for? To which most women will rather indignantly say, 'I wear it for myself', whether or not that's true, because it seems like the right answer to give. No woman wants to admit that she's doing anything for a man for fear of being branded shallow, superficial or, worse still, a slut (it does happen, we are mean to each other).

I'm sure the 'wear it for myself' position is the right answer. Yes, I may be doing it so I look better; no, I probably wouldn't wear it if I was guaranteed to be in my house all day, but if I'm not wearing it I don't feel very attractive, and whether that's right or not, it's the truth. I wear it for myself because I *normally* don't think I look very good without it. If I were to go out on a date I would of course pile it on, to make me look and feel as attractive as possible. And while this may seem to be an act saved for the man I'm courting, it actually isn't; it's something I'm doing for me so that when I spend time with him I feel as confident as I possibly can, safe in the knowledge that I look my absolute best.

Lots of women argue that we're made to feel we need to apply make-up for men. One woman told me openly that her husband often used to tell her he preferred her to wear it (a cardinal sin if you ask me, and hopefully the reason they're no longer married) but I don't believe that to be the case in most instances.

Most men just don't understand you. My boyfriend, for one, describes you as war paint. Something totally apt, to be honest, as you do help me deal with daily battles, but he really wouldn't notice if I'd contoured, what palette I'd used on my eyes or if I'd tinted my eyelashes. It's worth remembering that in the eighteenth century, England nearly passed a law allowing husbands to divorce their wives if they caught them wearing make-up. Yes, times have changed, but let's face it, parliament was hardly brimming with women in those days, and this decision came from the men, for the men. They didn't care for make-up then, and I'm not convinced they care for it massively now.

There is a chance, however, that women are wearing make-up for the sake of other women. Well, I say a chance, I mean an almost certainty. You know earlier, when I said that girls were mean? I wasn't lying. It's worth remembering that us women, whether we'll admit it or not, are always in relentless competition with other women. Much like men often find themselves resorting to their primal instincts, feeling the need to compete for the best mate, provide for their families and wave their willies around, isn't it instinctive for women to make themselves the most attractive of the herd? Probably. And that's where you come in, I suppose . . .

It's all very confusing, to be honest. I love the idea that at all-girls' schools no one feels the need to wear make-up, and I've spoken to a number of girls who attended them and said that, no, they didn't wear it when they were at school, which is great. But if the film *Wild Child* is to be believed, then my friends were either wrong or in the minority, as it would seem to suggest that pupils at these schools probably should wear make-up at all times, just in case Alex Pettyfer shows up. (Spoiler alert: in a school packed full of barefaced girls, Pettyfer only takes interest in the new girl, a super-glamorous American who is the only one to use you. It's also worth knowing that all the other girls miraculously have their first kisses upon being introduced to you.)

Is it the case that male directors deemed this to be a plausible plotline? Or is it because tall, hunky blond men are only attracted to dolled-up women? Or is it that Emma Roberts felt she could only get the man because, thanks to her make-up, she was the most attractive of the pack? I don't know for sure, but what I do know is that the fact Emma's character got the guys AND mastered winged eyeliner was not a coincidence. True, in the end her personality won him over, but it wasn't her sense of humour that caught his attention in the first place.

But that's a different problem entirely. Regardless of who we are wearing you for, the one thing that comes up time and time again is the belief that girls have been introduced to you far too young. As one wise mum once told me: 'Make-up is for grown-ups, like smoking, swearing and shaving your legs', but really, how do we control this? There are the extreme cases, as are found in American beauty pageants, but more worrying are the ones that happen every day, that are going unnoticed. The girls who haven't even started their period but who feel the need to wear you; the ones who haven't even got spots to hide caking themselves in foundation. But what chance do they stand? EVERYWHERE they look, they see you. On Mummy's face, in their teacher's handbag, in every magazine, advert and newspaper that uses photos of musicians, politicians and actresses – all of them wearing make-up. I mean, for God's sake, a survey conducted in 1991 revealed that female politicians who hired a Hollywood make-up artist were 30 per cent more likely to win elections. Imagine that statistic now, twenty-five years later, in a world where Kim Kardashian can publish an entire book of photographs of herself, you guessed it, made up to the nines. Our prime minister wears make-up every day. How can you tell a young girl not to when the very woman she should be aspiring to above all others is wearing it every time she appears in public? It's impossible. 'If Mummy, Miss Elm, every woman in every film, the lady on the front page of the newspaper AND the leader of our country wears it every day then WHY CAN'T I?' – how do you answer that?

This is the problem you are going to need to prioritise. Because the fact of the matter is these girls don't need to change themselves; they're too young to bow to the pressures of society, or so I would have hoped. At the end of the day, your sole purpose in this life is to create a false representation of beauty, whether or not you mean to. Together with your friend, air-brushing, you are wreaking havoc on our beauty standards. To use you to enhance our natural beauty is one thing, but to use you because we aren't happy the way we are? That's quite another.

One of my closest friends broke my heart when she
told me that she hates 'not wearing make-up when I meet
someone new'. I almost feel that I have to say, 'I can do
better!' When I asked her if she would be happier if all
make-up was just taken away, she replied, 'I feel no one
would be attracted to me.' And this really stresses me out
because this came from one of the most beautiful women
I know, someone you would never assume to have any
insecurities and one that, since I lived with her for five years,
I can tell you looks perfect without any make-up on.

So. What are you going to do about it?

We know you're not going anywhere ever. We love you
too much. We have also sadly established that so many
women need you in their lives, so a boycott isn't going to
happen (you can breathe now, your $170-billion industry is
safe), but something needs to change.

Women only consider themselves beautiful when they
are perfectly made up, and this has everything to do with
the fact they've been taught to look at themselves in an
unappreciative way far too young. So what I'm going to
need you to do right now is take a back seat for a while. Do
what you've got to do in the average handbag, act as you
would normally on the face of every worker-bee, but please,
for now at least, ease up in your involvement in making
the 'perfect' woman. In real life there isn't one, and you are
helping to create a picture of something that isn't real.

I still love you – hell, I'd go as far as to say that I need
you – but I don't want that to be the case anymore. I don't
want this pressure; I've had enough. Thank you for all you

do, thank you for allowing me to feel better about myself, and thank you for making me feel beautiful. But please remember what I said. I know you can't talk, but next time an eleven-year-old reaches for you in the aisle of a shop, please ask the loo rolls to make a commotion and distract her because, whether you like it or not, you are creating a whole ton of problems for that girl that can definitely wait a few years.

See you in the morning, I guess,

Em xxx

Dear L'Oréal

Thanks guys, you're right: I am worth it.

Em xx

Dear 'Thinspiration'

cc #bodygoals #beachbodyready and that bloody #thighgap

Do you know what it would take for me to have a thigh gap? A proper, knees-together, thighs-apart thigh gap that doesn't just happen because my joints are all weirdly hyper-mobile? It would take surgery. My pelvis is too small, or my legs are too big, or something, I don't really know which, but I know with absolute certainty that there is no natural way in which I could create a gap between the very tops of my thighs. I also know that I will never be thin. I could be slim, I am relatively slim, but I will never be *thin*. I wasn't built that way. I have bosoms, rather large ones. I have muscles in my arms and legs that I rely on to get up all the stairs to my house and to stop my dog from dislocating my shoulders. I have an enormous father and some of his genes. I probably would have made quite a good swimmer had I ever been honest to my teachers about my monthly cycle. And you know what? For the first time in a very long time I am TOTALLY OK with that. But it hasn't always been like this. In fact, until very recently, it has been absolutely nothing like that at all.

Do you know what I used to wish for when I was younger? Wish for more than anything in the world? I used to squeeze my eyes shut, cross my fingers (on just one hand because if you did it on two it would cancel the first wish out) and wish that when I woke up in the morning I would be thin. I did this every single night. I would lie in bed reading magazines and I would look at photos of women in bikinis in *Heat* or *Closer* or see women in films or TV shows and I would hope against hope that when I woke up I would look just like them. I would look around at my classmates, all of them so much thinner than me, and wish that I had their bodies. Did it occur to me that the reason so many of them were so 'thin' was because they hadn't hit puberty and grown boobs or hips yet? No, of course not; all I saw was ironing board upon ironing board and I'd curse my body for not looking like theirs. I thought if I prayed for it hard enough it would happen.

I would imagine how it would be in the morning. Along with my fat, gone too would be my wardrobe and I would have a whole new one full of T-shirts that flashed my midriff and denim jeans that made my legs look like they went on for days. I'd imagine myself finally saying yes to a party at school and I would get all dressed up and walk in and all the boys would fall at my feet. I had images of myself on the beach in far-off climes posing in between equally beautiful friends for endless photos and then putting them on Bebo and then my Facebook page for my (numerous) friends to all 'like'. I would have SO MANY likes. I wished for this life so hard, it was all I wanted.

Around this time *Gossip Girl* had just come out and Blake Lively, or Serena van der Woodsen, as she was then, was the girl I NEEDED to be. A figure I could only dream of, a wardrobe that was beyond comprehension and hair that was just SO amazing. Hair, I ought to say, that was quite unlike mine, which was at this point short, a funny purple colour and frizzy as hell. I imagined all the things that would just be so much easier if I had a flat stomach; how much more interesting I would be and how many more friends I would have. I was utterly convinced of it, to the point where it became a fixation.

Every day I would look at my reflection and grimace. Sometimes I would look at it and cry. I would grab fat rolls on my stomach and squeeze them together so tightly there were finger marks there when I stopped. After I read one of the *Angus, Thongs and Full-Frontal Snogging* books at my prep school, I learned that a woman should not be able to see over her boobs; that when she looked down she should see nothing but boob then floor. Maybe occasionally a little bit of foot if she was standing at a weird angle, but never stomach, you should never see stomach.

After I read that I don't think I breathed out for an entire month. When I went away to big school (just as the *Gossip Girl* obsession started) there were times when I was so unhappy that after eating I would cry to the point where I was sick. I wouldn't call what I had bulimia. It wasn't bulimia, it was just unhappiness, which thankfully didn't last long and stopped before I had time to even tell anyone about it, let alone develop a problem. Well, that sort of problem anyway. This was a problem, of course, but one of a different kind.

It can't have happened more than a handful of times but the constant unhappiness, the insecurities, the stomach-grabbing and fat-hating? That seemed to go on for years to the point where I can't remember when it stopped. It has only been very recently, since I turned into the woman I am today, that I've found myself able to say with full confidence that I am happy, properly happy with my body, for the first time in twenty-three years. And that can't be right. But do you want to know the worst part about all this? The worst part was that I never told anyone how I was feeling – because being 'fat', not having a 'thigh gap' or an enviable body . . . well, it felt like my fault.

To this day, I have never told a soul about any of this. Writing these words now I am close to tears, heartbroken for my younger self and for the fact that I handled this all on my own, for all of those years, because I thought it was *something that happened to all teenage girls.* Or something that was just *supposed* to happen to this one at least. Sure, my friends didn't seem to have the same hang-ups as I had, but then again why would they when they were the proud owners of the bodies I wanted so desperately? I didn't see any of this as a problem.

I don't know when this changed, when I saw the light or when I realised my legs were much more use to me when they lived together rather than inches apart, and that my stomach rolls actually provided fairly impressive insulation in the winter. Perhaps it was after I started the blog, or maybe it coincided with leaving school and growing up, but I'm thankful that it did, because I can now say with absolute confidence that I love my body. Even the bits that I hate, I love. But it took me SUCH a long time to get to this, and after everything that teenage Em went through, staring at women I deemed 'perfect' because society showed me photos of them day in, day out, I finally see you for what you are: beauty ideals, 'thinspiration', the thigh-gap ... I see you as pure fucking evil.

Did you know that on average one in every 250 women has anorexia? Well, you ought to; you helped them get there. But did you know that an overwhelming amount of those suffering are teenagers and that some cases have started in children as young as six? Yes, I bet you knew that too, because you're there, aren't you? Just waiting to help them on their merry little way to self-destruction.

OK, let's try it another way: are you happy with your role in society right now? Because I'm not. And do you want to know the thing I'm angriest about in all of this? I am so angry that you were made by people. That actual, living, breathing human beings not only created you, but watered you and nourished you until you became what you are today. And not just any people either, no – the worst thing about all of this is that you are a concept dreamed up by women, for women, simply to fuck with women. It's a widely known fact that most men prefer a woman with 'a bit of meat on the bones', that Kelly Brook would beat Keira Knightley to 'Rear of the Year' time and time again, and that the majority of guys would more readily assume a thigh gap was a chicken-based fast-food chain than a target for hordes of insecure women.

On the whole, we are NOT doing this for men; men have nothing to do with this. (NB. I know there are some men out there who prefer skinnier women. I am also aware that a lot of women get very thin as a result of unhappy relationships and that sometimes men can play a big part in unhappy women 'achieving' this goal. But that is not what I am referring to in this instance.) In fact, men's role in 'appreciating' women only helps to highlight the juxtaposition between the two categories we are ultimately trying to fit into: sexy and sophisticated. The 'Rear of the Year' winner Kelly Brook has no doubt been ogled by many a man, but does that in turn make her cheap? Keira Knightley, in stark contrast, falls into the ranks of 'sophisticated', since she is not necessarily considered an object of lust, which leads us again to another decision. What do we want to be? And do we have a choice? Does a curvy body mean we have to slot into one, whereas a taller and slimmer frame puts us in another? If the fashion industry is to be believed, then that is definitely the case. But although we can use men to make this point, their involvement starts and ends with their testosterone as, after their initial interest, this becomes another area in which us women find ourselves striving once again to get one over on each other. We are doing ALL of this because we are in competition, or admiration, of other women. This was our idea and this is now our problem. And it's a big one.

Thanks to someone deeming that this was something to aspire to, that *you* were something to aspire to, we have been made to feel like our bodies aren't good enough. That the thighs we rely on to get us through our morning commute on the bike are 'too big'; that the breasts we use to feed our children are 'sagging' and that our midriffs, containing a substantial amount of our vital organs, are 'fat'. Being natural is such a rare and scary thing for a woman these days that we forget what we are SUPPOSED to look like, and that, of course, is ourselves. But really, guys, what chance do we stand? We don't see people like us in the media anymore and, if we do, they are getting a battering for being 'too fat' or 'too old'. So we are left to compare ourselves to women who are built entirely differently. Who don't eat like we eat, who exercise more than we have time to, who have professional make-up artists and hairdressers on tap, who are often cast because they are five-foot nothing to make the male actors appear bigger. When we are constantly comparing ourselves to something so *fake* how are we possibly able to then love ourselves? We can't, it's impossible.

Time and time again you see that *normal* people just don't make it as role models anymore. And even if they're 'normal' when they're starting out, as I suppose everybody is at the beginning, you can be rest assured that within a matter of weeks their Instagram accounts will have been weeded through, with unflattering images deleted, they will have their teeth fixed ASAP and a radical haircut, before the inevitable diet is started and the personal trainer is hired. I can't even blame them; there's so much that if I had the money I would fix about myself, but that right there is the problem, isn't it?

Do you remember when Little Mix broke onto the scene in 2011? They were virtually unrecognisable as the clones

they are today. (I know I'm sounding a little bitchy, but
SERIOUSLY?!) Most notably different of course is Jessy, the
girl who was known to us while on *X Factor* as 'the fat one'
because she was, like, *one dress size bigger than the others*, who,
unsurprisingly, rather than staying at her beautiful, natural,
curvier size, lost a whole ton of weight so that she wouldn't
stand out in the line-up. Then of course we could look at
Adele, still a curvy girl by anyone's standards, but a whole load
smaller than when she came to public attention in 2008. It's
the same story with Scarlett Moffatt from *Gogglebox* and 2016's
I'm A Celebrity Get Me Out Of Here winner – a girl who gained
a little bit of fame on a reasonably popular TV show (the sole
purpose of it being to show *normal* people at home watching
telly), who is now literally and totally unrecognisable. She
clued-up pretty quickly and realised that if she was going to
make a success of herself then she needed to lose weight, and
lose it quickly. It's the same story everywhere.

Looking at society circa 2017, the picture is a tragic one.
You can't be a famous 'fat' woman unless you:

- Are literally the most talented human being on the
  planet, e.g. Adele.
- Are willing to be defined as 'the fat friend' in every
  film, e.g. Rebel Wilson.
- Are prepared to not be fat anymore and have a
  fitness DVD coming out in time for Christmas, e.g.
  Charlotte Crosby.
- Are a stand-up comedian, in which case it's basically
  mandatory, e.g. Jo Brand.

You can't be on primetime television and not be conventionally pretty unless you are:

- Over fifty, e.g. Anne Robinson.
- Really funny and prepared to laugh at the fact that you're not pretty, e.g. Miranda Hart.
- Prepared to have lots of work done, e.g. Sharon Osbourne.

So let's draw a quick comparison and look quickly at the men, shall we? You can't be a famous fat man unless you are:

- Seth Rogan
- Jonah Hill
- James Cordon
- Jeremy Clarkson
- Sam Smith
- Zach Galifianakis
- Eric Stonestreet

Oh wait . . . You CAN be a famous fat man. And be the lead in films. And have your own late-night chat show. AND not just be identified as the fat man. Oh well, that seems fair.

Mind you, at least there aren't hundreds of men that aren't conventionally attractive on our TVs every night, unless of course you count:

- Rowan Atkinson
- John C. Reilly
- Elton John
- Steve Buscemi
- Mike Myers
- Jack Black

Huh. As it turns out you can also be an 'ugly' male celebrity. In fact, there are hundreds of them. 'Cos looks don't *really* matter when you're a man, do they? Not if you're funny, or if you're rich.

I'm not saying that men have it super easy – of course they don't. But, beauty ideals, tell me this: why is it I couldn't stop thinking of overweight famous men when I struggled to think of more than three women who fell under the same umbrella? Why is it that men are able to continue being great actors given great roles late into their forties and they're not asked to merely be either an old character or the parent of the lead? Why are you saving all this sexist pressure for us women? Don't you think we've got enough to deal with?

Do you know what happens if you type the words #thighgap into Instagram? This message comes up: 'Posts with words or tags you're searching for often encourage behavior that can cause harm and even lead to death. If you're going through something difficult, we'd like to help.' Which was a message I was relieved to see, albeit a little surprised. It would seem that this problem has at least been acknowledged to a degree by the powers that be at planet social media. After that, however, there is a little button that says 'show posts', and so anyone on the hunt for a real incentive not to eat dinner tonight is able to completely disregard the warning and carry on as normal.

Nice try on Instagram's part but not really enough, was it? Because once in, once past the warning, you're exposed to hundreds of thousands of images of women. Some are documenting their recovery but lots of them, most of them, are sharing photos of unbelievably frail-looking bodies with messages from girls who are asking for help to lose more weight. Most of them are #thinspiration to others with anorexia who are thinking about giving up. Most of them are from girls who are beating themselves up for eating more calories than they've burned in a day. Most of them are girls celebrating the fact that they are in pain. That they are hungry. Because it's working, because they are now #bodygoals.

Instagram has now banned the hashtags #thinspiration #probulimia and #proanorexia, which is of course a step in the right direction, but unfortunately not enough, as even by typing in #ana, you are instantly able to look at 300,000 plus of the same images, just rebranded. Images that are going unreported and pretty much unnoticed by the millions of other social media users.

From where I'm sitting, Instagram seem to be serious about this, which seems a little ironic given that you can't show a female nipple under any circumstances (mastectomy scars included) due to their nudity rules. Even more ironic when you think that Instagram's big brother Facebook

actually banned a photo of so-called plus-size model Tess
Holliday from its site last year because, and I quote: 'Ads
may not depict a state of health or body weight as being
perfect or extremely undesirable'. The image of the model
in a swimming costume was not allowed because it 'made
viewers feel bad about themselves'. It seems that you can be
too fat for social media, but too thin? The jury is still out on
that one.

So there you are, in all your glory, beauty ideals. Not only
helping good, hard-working, honest women feel like shit day
in and day out, but helping to fuel an illness that is literally
helping more vulnerable women and ill young girls to starve
themselves to death. How are we letting this happen? How
do you seriously, legitimately, exist in this world? How do
we let you be here? How, as STRONG women, the ones
out breaking balls, being prime ministers, running for
president of the US, marrying each other, starting our own
companies, are we ALLOWING this to even be a thing?
Allowing YOU to tell us what we should look like? That
we're not good enough. That we need to be 'thinner than
a piece of paper', that we need to be an 'hourglass', that we
shouldn't be a 'pear', that we should have a 'thigh gap'? How
are we letting this big, omnispresent power that is the beauty
ideals rule our lives? We can't look in a magazine without
seeing a size zero model. We can't walk down the street
without passing an advert for a diet pill and we actually have
to battle through streams of sponsored posts full of someone
telling us how to better ourselves if we actually want to SEE
anything on social media in any capacity.

What is the ideal woman anyway? Is she five feet, eight inches? Does she have long, glossy, healthy hair? What colour is it? Brown? Blonde? Or does it depend on her complexion? Which is . . . caramel? English rose? Black? What bra size is she? A DD? Or is that slutty? Probably. Maybe a 30C? How big are her lips? What shape is her nose? What colour are her eyes? How big is her arse? Tell me who to aspire to here. Is it Megan Fox or Kim Kardashian? Cameron Diaz or Mila Kunis? Or Michelle Kegan? Or Jennifer Lawrence? Because those are all very different women but each has won various sexist competitions that have deemed her to be perfect in some capacity. What makes her so? Which direction am I supposed to go in here? DO YOU NOT SEE HOW CONFUSING THIS ALL IS?

The truth is there is no one ideal woman; she comes in different shapes and sizes. Supermodels are perfect, they're six feet tall. The Kardashian crew are also perfect. But they're all tiny, at five-foot-one or thereabouts. Hair colours are all different, boob sizes, eye colour – they're all different. Perfect comes in many forms, it would seem . . . yet it isn't me. Nor will it ever be. To you, beauty ideals, I will never be perfect. There will always be something I can improve on. I have an overbite. I have cellulite. My teeth are not blinding white. I'm the proud owner of bingo wings. When I pull my head back it gives me such a double chin that you'd be forgiven for thinking my face was being squished into dough. My knees bend inwards. I'm on the cusp of having in-growing toenails. My hair is dry. But even if none of that was the case, I STILL wouldn't be perfect. I will never be perfect, and at this point I find myself feeling sorry for those people that try.

Every day I see articles in the *Daily Mail* or interviews with reality TV stars on *This Morning,* who come forward to talk about why they got a nose job, why they've lost six stone, why they had fillers done, why they've changed their hair so 'drastically', and time and time again the answers are the same: 'Because they weren't perfect before.' 'Because I've always been self-conscious about it.' 'Because people always made comments about it.' The women we are aspiring to, and looking up to, are being driven and pushed to better themselves too – in new, more extreme ways – by us.

And you know what? I've had it. I'm done. With all of it. No, you bastard things, my body may not be 'perfect', I may not have the glossiest hair or the thinnest legs. I might not be #bodygoals or have washboard abs. But my body is MINE. It's the equipment I use to get me through life. It's how I'm MEANT to be. I am meant to have wonky eyebrows and a thin top lip. I am meant to have strong legs and be covered in moles. I am meant to have funny-coloured eyes and I am sick to death of you telling me this is not OK. Sure, I colour my hair and go to the gym, but don't you dare, even for a minute, assume I'm doing it for you. I'm doing it for ME. I am DONE conforming to you. I am done with you telling me I'm not good enough, because I am. We all are.

There isn't a woman alive who isn't perfect in her own way, but there isn't a woman alive who would believe that either. Give a woman a compliment and you can be fairly sure she won't take it. Because you, beauty ideals, you, thinspiration, have made her feel that she doesn't deserve that compliment; that she isn't worthy of it.

> Em: Oh, my God, Sophie, you're looking so, so good, you've lost weight!
>
> Sophie: ARE YOU JOKING? I literally ate like a troll this weekend, all the sandwiches – *nomnomnom ahahaha* – I haven't lost weight.
>
> Em: Shut up, you DEFNITELY have.
>
> Sophie: No no, I literally haven't, it's just because I'm wearing black jeans! Love these jeans so much, they're so flattering, it's not me, I haven't lost weight, it's for sure the jeans.

An actual conversation I had with my friend this afternoon. A conversation I have every afternoon with all my friends who don't feel they deserve nice things said about them because they are told time and time again – and have been from the second they're old enough to understand – that they aren't good enough. And it's time for you to stop. Enough. Is. Enough. It's time for every single woman to look at herself and smile – to be told she looks beautiful and BELIEVE it. To go back for seconds and thirds and fourths of pudding if she wants to because she is safe in the knowledge there won't be a big yellow poster confronting her on the tube in the morning asking if she is Beach Body Ready. It's time for you to go now, beauty ideals, thinspiration and definitely you, you fucking little thigh-brow bastard you.

You were dreamed up as some sick little fantasy by a collection of women I want to slap. But that's all you are – you are a fantasy and for a long time you were mine. But not anymore. I'm my own fantasy now and quite frankly you can just fuck off.

Yeah, I went there. Don't contact me again.

Very nasty regards,

Em

Dear The Gym

I remember the first time I came to visit you. I was at school, and I was finally of an age where it seemed legit cool to say to my mates, 'Oh yeah, no, sorry, I can't come actually, I've got to go to the gym.' I must have been about sixteen, and this was a big old deal. Never one for competitive sports – unless you count the 14Es netball team to be something worth bragging about – I'm pretty sure I thought the gym was the place where I was going to thrive.

I knew I didn't like running, that my hand-eye coordination was truly appalling, and that at times the one sit-up that was me getting out of bed in the morning was a struggle, but I was sure the gym was going to be the place in which I flourished. I was almost 1,000 per cent sure that running on the treadmill was easier than running outside (because women in films always managed to do it with such ease) and that the cross-trainer was going to be the answer to my life's problems. I was confident I was going to fall in love with you and that within the space of just two short sessions I would be hooked, the weight I hated so much would fall off me and suddenly, thanks to you, the entire packet of chocolate digestives I'd eaten on the way there was going to be rendered irrelevant.

But of course, since we know jack shit about exercise in

this country, and because it is never once explained to us properly, I found out the hard way that none of this was going to turn out to be the case . . . not even close.

Unfortunately, thanks to the aforementioned overwhelming lack of physical education, I quickly discovered that the gym was not going to be my Mecca; rather, my Everest. Because no one had told me otherwise, here were some of the things I genuinely believed to be true, real-life facts:

- Calories were actual literal measurements of weight. There were 200 in my KitKat, so all I needed to do to make that KitKat OK was to sweat until the cross-trainer dashboard told me I had burned 201 and I would be in the clear.
- That if I did 100 sit-ups every night before bed, I would have a flat stomach and that area of my body had nothing to do with the food I was putting in it.
- That doing only the exercises I found easy (basically stretching on the mat) had the same benefits as doing the ones I liked less.
- That going only once a month was OK because it was one of those things that didn't need to be done all at once, and that my muscles wouldn't forget the journey I made forty-two days ago.
- That walking uphill on the treadmill was a better form of exercise than running.
- That five minutes on one machine constituted a workout. (I still sort of believe this to be true.)

No one told me that calories were a rough estimate and that my weight wasn't necessarily a reflection of my fitness. No one told me that a flat stomach is basically impossible to achieve, has a huge amount to do with hormones and requires aerobic exercise, good diet AND strength training. No one said that the reason I found certain exercises hard was because that was an area of my body that needed to be strengthened, or that if I went to the gym only once in a blue moon I might as well be pissing in the wind, as getting fit and strong required constant effort. So really, when you take all of that into consideration, are you surprised I failed SO many times before I succeeded?

When I was at school I think I convinced myself that I came to visit you a LOT. Looking back at it now, I understand why it seems that way. I was at a stage of my life where I wasn't being healthy, I wasn't a good weight and I knew I wanted to do something about it. I suspect that by going to the gym, no matter how infrequently, I thought I genuinely was. However, the gift of hindsight has shown me in no uncertain terms how catastrophically wrong I was getting it. Despite the fact that when someone looked at my body it definitely did NOT scream 'regular gym-goer', I was pretty sure that if I went enough – or at least told everyone I was going enough – and pretended I knew what I was doing, then no one would have to know the extent of my hopelessness.

I thought that if people saw me sitting on the mat rather than actually doing anything they would assume I was between sets; that if they noticed I'd been on the treadmill for only two-and-a-half minutes, then I was doing some sort of interval training (not that I knew what that was), and that if I put my towel over the front of the machine I was using then no one would know it wasn't actually turned on, in order to ensure as little resistance for my legs as possible.

I remember telling a boy who came to talk to me while I was on the treadmill that I was planning to do the London Marathon the following year (I wasn't, by the way – I hadn't applied and nor was I intending to) and the reason I was only going for a five-minute run that day was because I'd had a big run the day before and my (imaginary) trainer had advised I take it easy today. If he saw through this blatant lie then he never let on, and for that I'm very grateful. Unsurprisingly I never lost any weight or saw any indication that I was going to develop a visible muscle anywhere. But then again, I didn't really know that muscles were something I actually wanted or indeed or that I had to work for.

Fast forward five years and here we are. What can I say about our relationship that you don't already know? Often it feels very one-sided, but I suppose deep down we are probably friends. I pop in when I can – some months I'm in a few times a week, some months (most months), I'm basically pissing £57 down the drain because I can't face visiting and that's just that. And I don't even know how it happened, but somehow I went from total fucking rookie (complete gym failure) to a point where I'm preparing for my fifth cross-Europe bike ride, my second triathlon, and was actually genuinely disappointed that I didn't win the ballot to run the London Marathon. Honestly, thinking about it now, I really don't know how I got here, but I'm sure you had a big part to play in it, and not always a helpful one.

Because now ... now I don't mind going to the gym. Now I'm strong, and have at least a base of fitness to work from, I don't mind coming in. Because I sort of know what I'm doing, what I should be doing, what I'm good at and what I need to work on. I know that if I'm about to go on a long bike ride I need to get to spinning classes and strengthen my glutes and quads (after learning what they were because I genuinely had no idea). I know that if I'm going to get better at running then there really is nothing better for me than GOING FOR A RUN. And I know that if I want to tone up I need to use weights and do exercises I don't like, because they're the ones that actually work.

Now I know what I need to do I can ignore the beefcake blokes slapping each other on the back as they watch each other picking up ludicrously heavy weights before dropping them again. Now I know what I need to do I can step over the beautiful yoga-goers as they lie there on their mats looking exquisite. Now I know what I need to do I can ask one of the personal trainers for advice if I don't know how to work a part of my body. (Most recently I had to ask what triceps were and what I needed to do in order to get some. I know now they live on the arm and their absence is the reason so many of us have bingo-wings. I also learned that a couple of push-ups and a bit of weightlifting won't cause them to magically appear. They come about as a result of a fuck-ton of hard and ridiculous work; unsurprisingly I still haven't got around to making them.)

But let's face it; it's a bit of a bitch to do any of this stuff *before* you know what you need to do. You're not exactly an inclusive club, are you? It's a well-known fact that you make your money from the hordes of well-meaning, unhappy women who pledge to better themselves on 1 January only to discover by 2 February, when £60 is missing from their account, that their old life got in the way of their new one again. You're hardly found standing there with open arms inviting lost and confused newcomers into a warm embrace. Which basically means that if people aren't *already* fit when they come to you, then they're not going to bother coming at all. But how does anyone get fit in this country in the first place?

When asked, I say that I fell into exercise by accident, because it's true. Considering my less than impressive start, it's a miracle, really, and I count myself incredibly lucky that it happened at a young enough age. Most people who knew me from my schooldays genuinely cannot believe they're looking at the same girl – the one who opted to do badminton as her sport in sixth form because it required as little movement as possible; the one who now takes part in a triathlon every June.

'How did you do it?' they ask, and the answer is always the same: 'I'm not sure.' And I'm really not. Like the rest of the country, I pretty much had to go into all of this blind. If you weren't good at hockey or netball or running or rounders or hurdles (I DEFINTELY wasn't good at hurdles) at school, then you were pretty much left to wait for diabetes to make its move as far as the school was concerned. We

were left to our own devices (always irresponsible when
dealing with teenage girls) and as a result I left big school
with as much sporting know-how as I had when I'd left
kindergarten – with a 'thanks for taking part' prize for my
efforts in the egg-and-spoon race. No one had explained
aerobic exercise to me, or strengthening techniques or what
RPM or BPM were. It was like if you weren't a prodigy then
you weren't the school's problem.

Looking back, with hindsight I actually think it was rather
admirable that I was taking steps to better myself, however
pathetically, in the gym after school and, really, it's hardly
surprising that I failed. The fact that ANY English person
who is not the next Jessica Ennis gets any exercise done as
an adult, following the abysmal lack of physical education in
this country, is more than remarkable, it's a miracle.

So as I say to everyone, I fell into exercise quite by
accident. My mum asked me when I was eighteen and
incredibly unfit (during my lying about the London
Marathon stage) if I would be up for joining one of the Help
for Heroes bike rides the following summer, which would be
420 miles from Paris to London. I said yes without thinking,
still very much in my 'I've been to the gym at least five times
this year, I *must* be fit' stage, and before I knew it the ride
was three weeks away and I was anything but.

I somehow managed to pull that one out of my arse (much
more to do with the strength in my head than the strength in
my legs) and really haven't looked back. In doing that ride I
realised for the first time in my life that actually, when done
right, exercise could be quite fun and that, unbelievably, the

more I did it the easier it got. But I'm painfully aware how lucky I am to at least have what little fitness I do have. (Come wintertime I really am the laziest mo-fo in town.) Because I now know that starting from scratch in the world of fitness is probably the hardest thing you can do.

To my mind, one of the biggest problems facing people who want to better themselves through the medium of exercise – other than the aforementioned overwhelming lack of physical education we receive – is the gymtimidation (legit a word) that most people, usually women, feel when they're met with the prospect of seeing you. (For anyone not familiar with 'gymtimidation', it's basically the overwhelming fear of judgement you anticipate either before or during a gym session.) How else do you explain the fact that when Sport England did a survey in 2014, they found that two million fewer women than men partook in sport and exercise regularly, despite the fact that of those 9.4 million (MILLION!), 75 per cent of them (7.1 million) said they would like to be more active? You will of course argue that it's not your fault. But I'm afraid, as it transpires, it is: most women, when asked to give a reason as to why they don't exercise, said it was because they were afraid of being judged for either how they looked or for not being very good at what they were trying to do.

And are we surprised? No, not really. When I walk into my gym it's chock-a-block with people who seem to know *exactly* what they're doing. They're using weights in a complicated way, sweating like animals on treadmills and actually just *looking* impressive. It's an often-made observation that many women are too afraid to go into the 'weights' side of the gym because that's considered to be the 'man side'. They're scared that if they were to venture over there they would embarrass themselves and get judged by all the men who are no doubt poised ready to offer direction or, if you're lucky, a sympathetic piggyback back to the Pilates mats.

It is of course not surprising either that the uniform we're encouraged to wear is not a favourite (So. Damn. Tight.) and that often acts as a deterrent. And then of course there is the judgement we receive from other women. The ones who look so good in that damn tight Lycra. I have written a separate letter to them; they're a huge part of the problem I'm talking about here and, for lots of us, make the gym the stuff of nightmares. If you wouldn't mind printing off a few copies and handing them out to the women who float into your gyms every morning looking like angels and smelling like candles, I'd very much appreciate that. I'll cc you in.

The idea of 'bettering ourselves' is something most of us want to do. If we're not having the living shit shamed out of us by an advert on the tube or in a *Daily Mail* article for being overweight and unfit, then we have to admit it to ourselves when we get to the top of a flight of stairs and need to stop for breath.

And it's great that we have this tool on hand so close by, in the shape of you, to help us on our journeys of self-improvement. Except you don't really help. In fact, I think you might be the reason most of us have left it so long. We want to go to the gym because we don't like our bodies, but then we can't go to the gym because we don't like our bodies. Not only can we not win, it just isn't fair.

Imagine if other institutions took this attitude. Imagine if you got sick and called the doctors' surgery to be told they could help, but you can't come in if you're ill. Or if you were naked and needed to buy some clothes, but all the shops told you that you couldn't come in unless you already had some clothes on because they didn't accept naked people? Nothing would get done, because it just doesn't make sense, and yet still you exist – a total anomaly in society.

We're living in a weird little world at the moment. On the one hand everyone I meet seems to be doing triathlons every other weekend and is literally pissing protein powder, but at the same time everybody else seems to be succumbing to the obesity epidemic. Take my parents, for example: on the one side I have my mother, who has thus far completed six Ironman competitions and countless other physical feats, and on the other side I have my father, who lives by the quote: 'Why run when you can walk, why walk when you can stand, why stand when you can sit and why sit when you can lie down?'

And that, right there, might actually be the problem. As long as these two groups are being asked to train together on a level playing field, then animosity is bound to build up. No doubt twelve-time Ironmen are not happy waiting for the likes of sixteen-year-old me to stop texting and get off the mat. But then the likes of sixteen-year-old me – who are busy lying on the mat psyching themselves up for the biggest sit-up of their lives – don't appreciate this beefcake looming

over them, eyeing them up as if trying to work out if they
contain enough protein to make a good smoothie, and
pressuring them to get a move on. But what are we meant to
do?

Well, thanks to initiatives such as This Girl Can, the gap
does seem to be slowly closing, which is great. But, but . . .
don't you for a minute think you've got away without
having to change your ways, because, I'm sorry, but this
scaremongering, this *gymtimidation* just isn't going to work
anymore. It's high time you guys got more inclusive. So
here's what I suggest, take it or leave it:

- Offer ACTUAL instructions on all the machines as
  to what to do with them (and not just drawings of
  muscly men with coloured-in orange bits to show the
  muscles you *could* have if you sat on there every day
  for the rest of your life).
- Have noticeboards around the gym with suggestions
  for what to do to exercise each part of the body.
- Have beginner classes separate to the normal ones
  for the people who really have to mentally prepare
  themselves to get to a class like this.
- Employ people to work at the gym who will not
  only smile at the customers who look like they're
  struggling but also offer to help them, rather than just
  spending all their time watching the impressive blokes
  bench however many pounds.
- Offer more classes in the dark. I did a 'spinning
  in the dark' class once at Virgin Active and it was

everything. No judgement, just me and the bike. I
loved it.

• Email your clients regularly with motivational
  quotes and actually good, useful advice. (N.B. Not
  motivational quotes written over super-toned, size 8
  yoga women doing the downward dog in front of a
  sunset. This will make us want to throw our phones
  out of the window.)

Oh, you know what . . . I think I might be onto something
here. Maybe I ought to open a gym. What d'you think, guys,
would you like me as your leader? For a branch of Pretty
Normal Gyms? Places that people actually enjoy coming to?
Where you're allowed to be shit at stuff without judgement?
Where people will help you get better? And explain your
bodies to you? Yeah. You know what, I might just do that.
Because right now you lot are doing far from enough, and in
a world where we *really* should be bringing everybody up and
helping them to love themselves and treat their bodies right, I
don't know how you are all getting it so wrong.

I suppose, before I sign off, I ought to say thank you,
for having me at my worst, and sorry for all the times I've
broken a bit of equipment. And I'm sorry for the time my
sister did an enormous fart mid sit-up and probably scared
away most of your clients. Sorry for that time I had to leave
a class midway through because my hangover was so bad
that the exertion made me vomit. I'm sorry for the time
my friend came to a reformer Pilates class after her work's
Christmas lunch pissed as a fart and broke your machine

falling off the carriage. And I'm sorry that I so often leave my horrid sweaty body-prints on the floor or the saddle. But those thank yous and sorrys are sort of half-hearted, because all I really want to say is: buck your ideas up! Because there are lots of women out here waiting to come in and they could really do with you opening your doors a little wider to make room for us all.

I look forward to seeing what you come up with,

Em

Dear Women Who Know They Look Good In Lycra

First things first, congratulations on looking so good in Lycra.

I understand this is far from the easiest thing in the world, and the fact you're pulling it off speaks volumes about your discipline and willpower. I also understand how hard you have worked to ensure you do, in fact, look this good in Lycra, and that as a result you feel the need to wear it as often as you can.

But before I carry on, I just need to ask you a few quick questions:

- Do you need to wear it to the school gates both when you're dropping off AND picking up your kids? Have you really, really, spent all day in the gym?
- Do you need to wear it to the pub? This is a place we come to drown our sorrows, not be shamed into feeling like a failure.
- Do you own anything else?
- Do you sleep in it?

I KNOW it's practical and that, yes, society has accepted it as full-blown appropriate outdoor, about-town attire now, and I know that you know you look amazing and you're much too busy doing that and living a very enviable life breeding perfect children and drinking spinach smoothies to get changed, ever, but for me, please try.

Because as much as I would love to be like you right now, as hard as I try I literally can't, for a few very legitimate reasons.

- I more often than not forget to shave and/or moisturise my legs, so this means that underneath my three-quarter-length running leggings, I end up exposing my revolting laziness to the world in the shape of two very scaly, hairy legs, which immediately prevents me from looking good in Lycra.
- I have a similar problem with my underarms. It's very boring to remember to do that every day and so, although I'm not 'hairy' as such, I'm often on the stubbly side, which is revolting and, again, prevents me from looking good in Lycra.
- I can't afford to buy matching kit. And even if I could, I don't think I'd be able to pull it off. Unless you are an ironing board of a woman, patterned trousers seem to enhance rather than detract from the problem. I also only have one pair of trainers (because foolishly I thought that was what everyone did) which I imagine would look grubby and offensive underneath my matching top, leggings and headbands and, as a result, that prevents me from looking good in Lycra.

- Sports bras do weird things to my boobs. I notice you ladies always seem to be sporting an impressive cleavage, something I don't and can't understand. By my understanding, the whole point of the sports bra is to 'strap 'em down', which instantly pulls me hugely out of proportion; once said device is in place, my stomach then protrudes further out than my boobs, which doesn't help me achieve the desired look and prevents me from looking good in Lycra.
- I can't master make-up appropriate for the gym. When I sweat (which is something that happens to those of us who aren't superhuman, resulting in beads of water forming at various places around the body), the make-up that was on my face either ends up on my shirt or on the nice white (WHY WHITE?!) gym towels provided, which of course prevents me from looking good in Lycra.
- My hair. HOW AM I SUPPOSED TO DO MY HAIR? I am incapable of creating 'sexy' hair at the best of times and then, after I've sweated (see above for description), it either straps itself firmly to my scalp or explodes outwards every which way it can. I have never, in my entire life, finished a workout with hair that should be seen (or probably smelt) by the public, which OBVIOUSLY prevents me from looking good in Lycra.
- Quite a lot of Lycra is see-through. My bike shorts are pretty much sheer (and at £30 a pop I won't be replacing those monthly, thank you very much) and

you're not supposed to wear pants with them. So
where does that leave me? No one exposing their
vagina looks good in anything, so on the material
alone I am prevented from looking good in Lycra.

- It's so damn tight. It's fine when I'm standing up (just
  about) but the minute I sit down it's like watching
  a collection of brightly coloured raw sausages being
  squished out between my miraculously flat bosom
  area and my see-through bottoms, which definitely
  prevents me from looking good in Lycra.

Do you see the predicament I'm in here? What am I
supposed to do? HOW DO YOU PULL THIS OFF? Give
me your secrets.

You know, I'm actually not even that angry with you.
I'm ashamed to say that I'm probably more jealous than
anything else. I've always wanted to be the type of woman
you seemingly are, and I know that's a terrible emotion that
doesn't look good on anyone, but you're killing me here. I
understand you've worked hard for this and that the gods of
all things great look down upon you with smiles and glitter,
and that is not your fault, but please, understand my plight.

I respect you for your dedication to your gym kit, but
perhaps the next time you come floating down the aisles of
Waitrose, smelling like a bath of Jo Malone, pouting slightly
as you deliberate between a chia seed and a raisin for your
lunch, spare a thought for me, the girl in the next-door aisle,
lusting over the Pringles. The one that smells more like a
changing room than a bath tub; the one who's the colour of

the tomato on top of the pizza she's just put into her basket (OK, who are we kidding, trolley), the one who, despite all of her efforts, can associate Lycra with one thing and one thing only: fear.

When people like me go to the gym it takes a lot of psyching up, a very good playlist and more determination than you can imagine, so when I begin my sloth-like lumber home after a less than impressive forty minutes of agony, I don't appreciate seeing you.

It's nothing strictly speaking personal, but for the good of all the insecure, hard-working, squishy women out there, please at least take the time to splash a little water on your face before you go out, as a nod to the world of exercise as much as anything else. Because no one, and I mean no one, believes you can look that damn good after a serious workout. And if you really, genuinely do, you're going to need to let me know how, so I can go and have a big old chat with the world to assess what I did wrong in my previous life.

Yours sincerely,

Someone who doesn't look that good in Lycra.

Em xx

Dear My Only Matching Set Of Underwear

Oh guys. I love the idea of you so much; I'm just so sorry that I can't embrace the reality. I want to wear you, I want to free you from the cupboard, I want to let you make me sexy and be the woman I'm so desperate to be, but I'm just not sure I can be arsed.

On the days I do manage to wear you, I'm convinced my life is going to change. I'm convinced that something massive is going to happen: that I'm going to be accidentally involved in a sex tape; that I'll feel compelled to give all my clothes to a homeless person and have to walk home in the nude, or that I'll get hit by a car and want to give the paramedics something nice to work on. Alas, it gets to 6 p.m. and none of these things have happened, and so at some point I gave up and just stopped wearing you.

I love the idea of being the kind of woman that wears you, and I hope that one day in the not-too-distant future I will be that woman. But right now? Right now I'm cool in the pants that lost their elastic in '09. Sorry, but also #notsorry.

See ya round someday, maybe.

Em X

Dear What Used To Be Food But Is Now Just Poison

I know you're terribly popular, so I don't expect you to remember me, but I LOVE you. We hang out a LOT, mostly at my house but sometimes we go out and about together as well. I'm often found skulking in the Free-From aisle of my local Co-op. You don't seem to like my house very much, as you never stick around for long ... any of this ringing bells? No worries if not, I just thought the tirade of abuse you're about to experience might be easier to hear if you feel it's coming from a friend.

This letter is for the lot of ya – from the stuff we find in Waitrose Organic all the way down to the Big Whoppers. It's for the Super Foods, the Curly Kale, the Trans-Fats, the Processed Sugar, the Gluten, the Carbs and the Calories. I want this to be read by all of you, up to and including your leaders, your smug know-it-all leaders ... the Nutritionists.

Tell me this: WHY, when I love you so much, do you treat me so badly? My love for you is unparalleled. I'm obsessed and relentlessly excited at the thought of you. I'm like a Labrador, so hungry and so loyal, and yet you repay me with the prospect of high cholesterol, weight gain, bad

skin, greasy hair, the threat of diabetes and IBS – that I
actually now have, thanks to you. Why do you do this when
I love you so?

And it's not just me. You're fucking with the lot of us
here. I mean, we literally NEED you to survive, you're
as crucial to us as air, but I'm yet to see people weirding
out about that. The process of putting you into our bodies
should, in theory, be as simple as breathing but we are
OBSESSED with you. We know what's good, we know
what's bad, and yet time and time again we get it wrong.

EVERYTHING needs you; you are everywhere,
imperative for the survival of all species. We're taught
early on about the food chain. We know that the early bird
catches the worm and, that it's a dog-eat-dog world. But
despite the fact we are more educated on the matter than
any of our animal counterparts, we're the only ones that
struggle with you. Have you ever heard of a lion freaking
out because tourist season is around the corner and he's been
a little excessive on the dentists? No, didn't think so. You're
equally unlikely to see elephants in the zoo fasting because
they want to look their best for the cameras. The rest of the
animal kingdom just seems to crack on with food; they need
it to survive, they eat it and that's that – but us humans? We
are fanatical about you.

I suppose a combination of our opposable thumbs and
advancements in technology have helped; gone are the days
of gathering fruits and catching what we eat, in Western
society anyway. The most foraging we ever need do is in
the discount section of our local supermarket. We're lucky

enough that food has never been made to feel scarce. I have never been on the brink of starvation and, as a result, I, like most people, treat you as a commodity to do with as I please. One way or another I've always known where the next meal is coming from – even if it's cold baked beans because I can't be bothered with anything else – and that's probably why it's all going wrong.

We have a choice, and choice is lethal to a greedy world.

Case in point: by all accounts sugar is actually more addictive than heroin, but for some reason completely beyond my understanding it's in everything we eat. We are well aware that sugar is bad for us, much like squirrels know which berries to avoid, but where the squirrels simply avoid the food that is poison to them, we fill our socks. Why? I have no idea.

Never once has my puppy asked me for a couple of sweeteners in her milk or a horse rejected a treat without icing on it, but everywhere we look human food is chock-a-block with bloody sugar. Why is it in everything? Why are we destroying you beyond recognition to actually give you the power to KILL us? And why has nothing been done? The present day's answer to heroin is as readily available as anything. In fact, thanks to the relentless offers in supermarkets, it's actively encouraged.

When my most recent tummy problem started up I had to give up sugar for a bit as part of my 'treatment'. It was only then that I realised *quite* how big a problem you are. Since I turned twenty I assumed that my sweet tooth must have fallen out, since I craved salty over sweet every time.

With that in mind, when I was told I had to give it up I didn't think it would be a huge problem. Wine would be a sad loss but my day-to-day eating surely wouldn't change that much, would it? Oh, my God. How wrong was I? It was the hardest thing ever. The withdrawals, the energy crashes . . . they damned near killed me. By the time this book comes out I hope to have sugar back in my life, but at the time of writing, thanks to this new diet, if I want to eat ANYTHING, and I do mean anything, I have to cook it from scratch.

Even things you would assume to be safe: salt and vinegar crisps, for example, have sugar in them. Bread, if I could eat it, has sugar in it. Everything has sugar in it. In my first few days without it I couldn't actually *do* anything because I was so exhausted. How had I let myself get to this point? How did I have an addiction that I didn't even know about? It happened when I wasn't looking and that's what worries me the most. Sugar is taking over our lives and we've hardly even noticed it happening.

I suppose one of the perks of a crystal meth addiction is that it's so hard to come by and so expensive you may find it easier just to pack it in all together. Oh, to be so lucky with you, you bastard thing! You're rarely more than a mile away from us and your manufacturers have ensured you're all-too tempting. I associate you with everything. At breakfast I'm thinking about lunch, at lunch I'm thinking about dinner, and at dinner I'm already thinking about tomorrow's breakfast. I never just go out and meet someone; we're always going out *for* something: for dinner, for lunch, or for coffee with a bit of cake. If I'm going to be out for the whole day I'll take snacks. I make all my plans around food. The idea of missing a meal honestly scares me.

And it's not just me. It's ALL of us. When we're not eating you we're talking about you, and when we're not talking about you, we're thinking about you. Food is E.V.E.R.Y.T.H.I.N.G. So maybe that makes us greedy? Or maybe we're addicted. Can you be addicted to something you need? Is that what bingeing is? Are we all just bingeing? How did it get like this? I simply don't know.

To look more closely at this issue I have decided to take you on a *Who Do You Think You Are?*-style adventure. Are you ready? Let's go.

Looking at your family history I can see that water and ice were the first to be discovered, followed by salt, oysters (who was the first person to think that snot-like substance was worth a try?), scallops, squid, octopus, insects, fish, frogs, mushrooms (someone will have had a giggle deciphering the good ones), greens, bear (although I wouldn't fancy my chances trying to kill one of those. I think I'd have looked for a rabbit first), venison, horsemeat, eggs and rice, amongst other things – all before 1700BC.

Over the next 10,000 years, grains and wheat were discovered, as was quinoa (so I don't know why the world is acting as if this miracle was just discovered). There was lard, wine, beer, honey, tortillas (?!), cattle domestication, milk, yoghurt, butter and olive oil.

And so it goes on, so that by the time Jesus was born there

was the wherewithal for a feast – although coffee was yet
to be discovered, so I'd have had little interest in anything
before the ninth century. (If I am to be reincarnated, gods,
please take note.)

New, normal foods continued to be discovered (although
at a slower rate) until 1922, which is when, I am guessing,
the foundations for the obesity epidemic were laid.

Look at this:

1923: Popsicles
1924: Frozen food
1930: Sliced bread
1932: Marshmallow sandwich cookies
1933: Chocolate-covered pretzels
1937: Krispy Kremes
1938: Waffles
1946: Nutella
1947: Betty Crocker cake mix
1948: Frozen French fries
1950: Frozen pizzas
1953: TV dinners
1964: Pop Tarts
1980: Chicken nuggets
1984: Redbull energy drinks
2013: Test-tube burgers (don't even go there…)

And so you became 'processed' when people started to
alter you from your natural state. And, as I'm sure is made
clear, modern food has been processed to shit. NOTHING

good (for our insides anyway) came out of the twentieth century. What with the Second World War, the space race and the pursuit of convenience, we saw the start of your demise. Say hello to spray-dying, juice concentrates, freeze-drying and sweeteners. And of course it didn't help that this shit was marketed to the middle-class working wives and mothers who, because they were busy working their asses off and fighting for their basic human rights, ate this shit up, which, although important, is definitely an argument for another day.

HOW DID YOU LET THIS HAPPEN? Our immune systems live in our gut but it feels like the guy who found that out just forgot to tell anyone about it. Would we still be so happy living off greasy fried food if we had grown up knowing that the thing that keeps us feeling well and BEING well resides in the same place as we're sending that Egg McMuffin? As of 2015, 70 per cent of calories in the US come from processed food. Which of course isn't helped by the fact that processed food is actually addictive. So, thanks to someone – or rather, thanks to our own stupidity and desperation for an easy life – we have driven ourselves to destroying you, so you are now found as a root cause of nearly all modern diseases, imbalances in our gut and are causing cancer and diabetes. Food is literally killing us. Dead. Murdered. WE ARE BEING KILLED BY OUR FOOD. And STILL we're eating you.

And it gets worse . . .

Reports show that silicon dioxide (sand) is found in canned foods and sodium bisfulite (LOO BOWL

CLEANING CHEMICAL) is used in crisps. And STILL we're eating you.

And on a personal note, ten years ago only one in 2,500 people world-wide were gluten intolerant; nowadays it's one in 133, partly due to more awareness, but partly due to the fact that modern grain has been modified into a monster I can't digest . . . so thanks for that.

To add serious insult to injury, if you bear in mind what we've just learned – about how I have to avoid sugar, that all food is basically poison – it's made worse by the fact that I have IBS, which means I'm intolerant to both gluten *and* dairy, which literally means if I listen to all the health stuff and to my stomach I can no longer eat anything.

If we're supposed to avoid sugar, which of course we are, that already cuts out half of your average supermarket. If you then take away all products with wheat in them and/ or cows' milk, you put me into a very small, very irritating, very expensive little box that I HATE. Actually, I hate it so much that I've written a separate letter where I talk ALL about it. I would suggest you read it.

Having said this, I do acknowledge that my stupid stomach is not entirely your fault and, in a bizarre sort of way, although this is by no means me saying that any of this is OK, I am incredibly grateful to it in lots of ways, as it has taught me so much about you that I otherwise wouldn't have known. It was only when I was told the bad news did I appreciate for the first time quite how gaping my knowledge was. The education in this country surrounding food is piss-poor. Same goes for America. I saw a clip the other day of Jamie Oliver going into a school in the USA and, I shit you not, the kids didn't know what a tomato was. Like, they literally had NO idea. How does this even happen?

Looking back at my childhood, I think I might have an idea. My logic growing up was as follows: if Mum's cooked it; it's healthy. If school is serving it, it's good for me. If I eat this quickly enough, it won't count. If I don't eat breakfast, I can have two lunches. I already feel fat, so one more cookie won't make a difference.

I was lazy and disillusioned and, as a result, a right little piglet. Just for your amusement as much as my own, I have decided to share with you an embarrassingly honest food diary installment from an average day at school for me (please judge silently and don't let me see the disappointment):

7.30 a.m.: Cocopops with grapes

10.30 a.m.: Three cookies eaten during first break

12.00 p.m.: Bag of Skittles eaten out of jacket pocket in lesson

1.00 p.m.: Lunch – for argument's sake, it was fish and chips

1.10 p.m.: Pudding

6.00 p.m.: Dinner – let's say shepherd's pie

6.45 p.m.: Snack – Chocolate Buttons, Quavers and strawberry laces

9.00 p.m.: Two pieces of toast with butter

And, OH MY LORD, I wish I was exaggerating but this was me in all my glory. I hardly exercised (although I liked to think I did) and I somehow still found it in me to complain relentlessly about how unfair it was that I never lost any weight and always had bad skin. Do you know how many calories are in all of that? I'm going tell you, and you're going to need to pretend it's no big deal, or I will probably cry: 2,742. I was eating 2,742 calories A DAY, easily. This is one thousand more than I should have been eating. And either nobody told me or I just chose not to listen, but either way it was not a good time.

I genuinely believe that if I hadn't developed my stomach problems I would never have had to face you for what you are and would probably still be living like that now. Because this doesn't suddenly stop when we leave school. I was under the impression that once I became a grown-up I would swirl around my big girl kitchen eating lots of curly kale, totally avoiding carbs and wearing trainers to work. This. Was. Not. The. Case. If anything it got worse because we added your dear friend alcohol into the mix. Take a look at what became a typical day for me once I got my first proper job out in the big wide world:

8.30 a.m.: Chocolate muffin (Caffè Nero. God I miss those!)

2.00 p.m.: Tuna baguette, Coke, grapes and chocolate cookie

7.00 p.m.: Cheesy pasta with wine and Jäger and vodka and cigarettes

Although only coming in at 1,906 calories (before the alcohol), there wasn't a single bit of nutrition going into my body. Everything I was eating was beige – delicious, but beige; no fibre, no vegetables, no nutrition, just shit. But in my defence I didn't know any better. I really did think this was OK, that I'd earned it; that because I was a grown-up I had to be getting it right; that because I bought it from a reputable shop, they must contain the right things. I'd see women sitting in GBK, burger in hand, without a fat roll in sight, and think, well, if she can do it then so can I. It never occurred to me that this was probably a treat, or that she had exercised that day or even that she'd had a salad at lunch.

I was never actually really fat; I was overweight, for sure, but miraculously I never tipped the scales and since the days of nothing but beige food I have lost a lot of weight – all of which I think I had to lose. But I don't think, as people often assume, that this was a result of my tummy problems. I think they were the catalyst that meant I clued up, did my research and discovered that, when treated right, you can be a truly great thing. Nowadays I know for example that it's good to start the day with protein, so I have two boiled eggs every morning for breakfast. I also acknowledge that fruit is essential, so I make a smoothie whenever I can be bothered, and I make sure that whatever I'm having for dinner, even if it's horrendously unhealthy, will be surrounded by a shit-ton of vegetables, because I have learned that when I eat better I actually FEEL better. I have more energy, better skin and I even poo more regularly (sorry, you didn't need to know that). This is not as a result of my forced diet, it's about the lifestyle I have chosen – but what annoys me is that we don't already just KNOW this. No one tells us the truth about it. Sure we're told to eat five-a-day and drink a lot of water but no one really tells us why. The reason we eat so much frozen pizza is because no one has shown us what great possibilities lie on the other shelves of the supermarket, or even what to do with them once they are in our kitchens. In theory, getting you right is the easiest thing in the world, but the reality is totally different.

I think this is why so many of us resort to dieting. We get you so wrong, so much of the time, and we can't understand there's a happy medium between starving ourselves and fitting a whole packet of chocolate buttons into our mouths in one go. As a nation we are incredibly overweight and a lot of us are very unhappy about it. It's not our fault, of course; we know basically nothing and so don't really stand a chance. So we diet. We get fat and then we're told that is bad. Then a nutritionist of some kind suggests a diet and, because we don't know any better, and since we don't want to be fat anymore, we diet. We live unhealthily for twenty-five days of the month and then resourcefully decide we will use the remaining five to start a diet. A diet that won't work.

As I write this we're coming to the end of 2016 and the talk of New Year's resolutions is extensive: who's giving up what, how much weight they plan to lose, how they will never eat sugar EVER again. We make all of these promises and have all of these expectations for ourselves and, ultimately, obviously, we let ourselves down – but in the moment we don't care; the promise of a diet is an excuse we use to binge like crazy over Christmas. Except, for most women, it doesn't just happen at Christmas; it's a thing that happens every Sunday. We sit staring at our plates piled high with roast potatoes, and tell ourselves it's OK because, come Monday morning, we're going to be 'good' again.

What does that even mean?

I hate diets. I hate the word even and I hope that you hate yourself for forcing people to resort to this ridiculous activity. I hate that because of you we drive ourselves into such a state of despair that we're willing to accept starvation as par for the course. Our punishment, it would seem, for enjoying you on a Sunday, is the promise that on Monday every morsel of you to pass our lips will be juiced.

I have never really 'dieted', not properly. I used to try when I was at school; I would give anything a go. Someone once told me that if I were to eat an apple before every meal my metabolism would speed up and I would lose weight. Unfortunately no one told me that in order for this to actually *work* I would need to stop putting sugar on my Cocopops. I mean, for God's sake; I was so totally clueless. It was not even that uncommon for me to place chocolate and grapes into my mouth at the same time in order to keep up the façade of healthy eating. Honestly, what the fuck? I would pass that off as a diet because I knew so little about it – why would I?

Growing up, I was aware that Mum had always 'dieted', so when I told her I was writing this I asked her about her

experiences – since, actually, I was so bad at dieting I didn't
feel qualified to comment. She told me she tried a whole ton
of stuff over the years but ultimately nothing really worked.
Although she'd lose weight initially, the following week
she would put it all back on again. I never noticed that they
didn't work; in fact, I don't think I even cared. I had no
interest in her diets and I just assumed it was something that
'adults did' and that it was a grown-up problem. It never
really occurred to me that they might just not *work* or that it
was hard for Mum to do it. I think I probably put diets into
the same category as periods – something that would happen
to me when I became a woman but not something I was
going to have to deal with for a while.

Of course, when I started secondary school that changed;
rumours inevitably flew around, hence the apple experiment,
but despite our best efforts, or mine anyway, it was always
going to be too hard to find the time to fill our boots with
cabbage soup. And so, while you were wreaking havoc
in many areas of many of my friends' lives in the shape of
disordered eating – binge eating, anorexia and bulimia –
there I remained with the idea of a diet still seeming
impossible to me.

The thing is, you, you bastard thing, should not be a
luxury or a commodity; you should not necessarily even be
something to fuck around with, and you certainly shouldn't
be something we're having to deprive ourselves of. I am fully
aware of the fact that your undoing is our fault, but that's
what makes it worse. You take the shape of a cauliflower, for
fuck's sake, what can we expect? You didn't stand a chance;

you could never have fought back. But WE, we should know better. You are an extraordinary thing, one we're taking for granted and taking the piss with at the same time.

If we stand a chance at getting back on track with any of this bollocks we need to take a good hard look at you, at your insides. Rather than just whining about the fact that sugar is going to ruin the world, and telling us to back slowly away from the Oreos, would it not make more sense to take you back to your roots? Surely you're up for that? You can't like existing the way you do now, can you?

I think the only way we're going to be able to handle this is if we clue up, and fast. I'll work on the education side of things for the kids of the future, and while I'm doing that you need to help me too. The next time someone tries to deep-fat fry you, perhaps ask them to stop and rethink it; when someone's coming at you with a huge bag of caster sugar, turn and run and, for the love of all that is good, will you please ask the vegetables to speak a little louder in the supermarket . . . get them tarted up a bit and let them know that if they're not ALL in someone's basket by the end of the day then there's going to be serious trouble.

If we work together I reckon we could be great, but you've got a LOT to do in the interim if we stand a chance of pulling it off. I'll be back to check on this, because the problem is getting worse by the minute and we haven't really got any time to waste.

I will not let the world be killed by its own monster. I won't let an industry totally controlled by human beings be our undoing. I can't.

I'm not even sure you've got ears but, if you heard a word I said, I'd be grateful for a reply.

Best wishes,

Em xx

Dear The People Who ACTUALLY Can't Eat Gluten ... Not The Ones That Just Don't 'Like' It

Hello, you poor sorry sods. I'm sorry to say that if you have just found out you can't eat gluten, your life is about to change forever. I got the news at the end of 2014, which saw me having to banish gluten and dairy from my life. Since beginning this letter I have subsequently had to give up sugar, caffeine and alcohol (although this isn't permanent, I hope) and so, since I totally understand the annoyance that is a restricted diet, I thought I should write to you to say that, although this is undoubtedly incredibly annoying and upsetting news, you will be OK.

Initially you will be hungry, you will be angry and you will be annoyed, but there are a few things you need to know if you stand a chance at getting through this. As I'm a seasoned veteran now, I thought I should share some of my secrets with you. First things first: you are going to need to prepare yourself for the three things people will ALWAYS say to you that you will make you want to rip your head off:

'Have you tried *Deliciously Ella*?' – to which the answer, from me at least, is always, 'Yes. Now fuck off.'

Now, newbie gluten-freer, please don't get me wrong. I LOVE *Deliciously Ella*. Well, I love the idea of it, at least. I firmly believe that what Ella has done with her life is beyond awesome and I am insanely jealous every time I see anything she achieves, because Ella has been on an incredibly inspiring journey, changing not only her life but the lives of countless others AND has the self-control and patience I can only dream of.

But heartbreakingly, I discovered I will never be anything like as amazing as Ella Mills. You will try several of her recipes, as I have in the past, and they will for the most part be undeniable successes. I recommend them; they're very yummy and easy and that's great, because you need all the inspiration you can get. You may however, like me, just not be BUILT for this healthy living. Let me give you an example: I took a leaf out of Hemsley & Hemsley's book the other day, and started spiralising. To my uneducated mind you could put a Mars bar through there and it would come out healthy, so for a good few months it was my go to appliance. On one of the early occasions, though, I learned that this healthy eating lark can actually be quite dangerous. I sat preparing my new and improved spaghetti bolognaise; but it wasn't until the courgette started coming through red that I realised my finger had somehow ended up in the mechanism. I don't know if this was a sign from God, or just an indication that I'm a twat but, either way, once this happened I reverted to buckwheat pasta, as you may do. There is no shame in it.

(There are very few kitchen appliances I still feel safe to

use. Aged fourteen, I stuck my hand into an electric whisk, just to see what would happen, and aged twenty-one – trust me, I wish it were younger – I burnt my hand beyond recognition on a piece of pitta bread straight out of the toaster. I'm honestly a liability in the kitchen.)

Brace yourself for the fact that when you tell people you can't eat gluten and dairy they'll assume you're some sort of health nerd (Ella, I'm afraid you've set the bar very high for us who aren't), but I need to make it clear that I'm not even close, and you probably won't be either. I can list all the pizza places in London that do GF and DF pizzas (Zizzi's, Pizza Express and Firezza for takeout), I am still obsessed with sausage sandwiches (GF obvi), and am basically a walking Snack a Jack.

Do not fall into the trap of assuming that you are now just going to become incredibly healthy; in most GF/DF stuff there is just as much sugar as in the normal stuff. The only reason you'll be any 'healthier' than anyone else is because you don't swell up like a balloon if you eat a loaf of GF bread, as opposed to a nice baguette. That and the fact you are now unable to partake in a fast-food binge at the end of a big night.

You will also not necessarily be any good at recipes; this is not a skill you automatically acquire with your diagnosis. I am not any good at recipes. I make great cookies simply by swapping flour for GF flour and butter for soya butter. This applies to everything, although I have been known to milk it in company (no pun intended), as you should, because it just sounds so much more impressive at a party.

I also make great cakes – like, stupidly good – but for some reason people assume that because I can eat them they must be good for you. This is not the case. I used to put so much sugar in there that you couldn't even taste what my cake was lacking. Do not think you can eat a whole cake and it won't count; it will count.

So although I would love more than anything in this life to be able to live by *Deliciously Ella*, I simply can't, because I am TOO LAZY. And most of the time I'm too broke. But mostly it's the lazy thing. You probably are too, and that is kind of OK.

'Ooh, I wish I was gluten and dairy intolerant, I'd be so thin!'

SHUTTUP.

This is the single most insulting thing that anyone will ever say to you, short of slagging your mum or making reference to your muffin-top. If this is something that a person is wishing for, then something is fundamentally wrong with their life.

I understand the appeal of this 'diet' – no, you can no longer eat all the things nutritionists tell you is bad for you, but trust me, I was perfectly able to replace all the bad things in my life with things that are just as terrible, that don't give me the shits.

I still smoke like a chimney. I can drink all alcohol, bar beer (which I never really liked anyway), and I can still eat chips, en masse. Yes, you may well lose a few pounds but, at the end of the day, you're the loser who has to watch everyone with their pizza while you're crying into your Caesar salad – served without the Parmesan or the dressing or the croutons, obviously. Yes, sometimes it really is that bad.

There is nothing enviable about this lifestyle. Implying otherwise is the MOST irritating thing anyone can say, so if someone does think it's appropriate to give it a mention, as a seasoned GF/DF-er I would highly recommend telling them to piss right off.

Kate Moss famously once said that 'nothing tastes as good as skinny feels', to which we say, NO. Nothing about salmon all the time tastes good; pretzels taste good, and I miss pretzels. You will too.

Please don't let anyone tell you they would wish for this, because it ultimately means that you're the dickhead at the party who has to turn down the hash brownies because they'll give you the shits and see you locked in the bathroom for the rest of the night . . . and no one wants to be that guy, not least because the best high in the world is not going to exempt you from the pain that comes along with gluten.

'Are you ACTUALLY allergic though?'

This question stems from the fad women living the fad lives who are on a fad diet, giving people like you and me a bad name. Here's what 'avoiding gluten because you're on a diet' means to people like us:

- We look like divas.
- No one wants to be the guy who orders a soya latte because you feel like a fool, following a trend you're not even sure who started.
- No one takes you seriously.

Do you know how many people have asked me if I'm *actually* allergic? The most common question waiters used to ask of me was, 'Please can we give you the bill because we need to close the restaurant now?' But as it turns out, it is without a doubt the predictably irritating 'Are you actually allergic or do you just not like it?' question. A couple of months ago I got asked this at a restaurant after we had firmly established there was nothing on the menu I could eat, as if the waitress was suddenly expecting me to say, 'Is there really nothing? Oh well, I guess for the sake of dinner I could break the rules. Ah, fuck it, I'll have the cheesiest pizza you can find, thanks.'

I can't do this because I AM ACTUALLY ALLERGIC and instead I had to eat steamed broccoli and boiled rice. I blame this on the 'fad lifestylers' who have made gluten-free eating seem like a choice when in reality there are lots of people for which it's a necessity; they owe us so much, and no one takes us seriously anymore.

The fear

There is always the fear that a chef is going to whack a bit of milk into the recipe just to make the thin posh girl fat (this may not describe you but thanks to the aforementioned fad

lifestylers that is the stereotype). Either that or they're going
to jizz in your sorbet because you're so difficult (I don't
think they actually do this, by the way but, I have to say, if
I owned a café in southwest London I'd be more than a bit
tempted). The threat is always there.

They will say all of this and more, a lot more. And it will
wear thin. Older people don't understand it because it simply
didn't exist in their day. It doesn't mean we're 'precious' or
'making it up' – it means they fucked up gluten for us with
pesticides and things, so don't for a minute let them give
you crap about it. It's a legitimate illness and it is not in your
head. It will get you down and make you feel crazy but don't
accept the eye-rolls or the 'why don't you just try it?' from
people who don't understand. You've got enough on your
plate (sadly, often not literally) and you don't need that shit
in your life. There are things you do need a lot of in your
life, however, and that is alternatives. There are probably
more out there than you first thought, although chances are
you won't have a flipping clue where to start looking. So just
in case you are starving right now and don't know what to
do, here's a list of some of my favourite gluten-free and cows'
milk-free foods that I pretty much survive on:

- Buckwheat flour
- Buckwheat pasta
- GF oatcakes (great 'cos they are sold
  EVERYWHERE)
- GF sourdough bread
- Snack a Jacks

- Meridian nut butters (*nomnomnom*)
- LoveLife GF/DF chocolate muffins
- Artisan du Chocolate goats' milk chocolate
- Artisan du Chocolate date chocolate (NO SUGAR EITHER!)
- Pomme Bears
- Alara muesli
- Black Farmer's GF sausages
- Free-From chocolate brownies
- Brown rice pasta
- GF pretzels
- Rude Health multigrain crackers
- Rude Health almond milk
- Basically Rude Health anything
- NOM Bars. The best snacks in town

They might find a 'cure' one day. Who knows? I wouldn't wish it on anyone, but you're here now, there's nothing that you can do about it, so let's crack on, shall we, as there will be plenty more annoyances along the way.

Everything you buy will cost double the price of what you bought before because the bastards know they've got you backed into a corner. You will miss out on a ton of insane taste bud experiences and you're going to become the most expensive date in the world because the safest option at most restaurants is the steak, but really, let's face it, you haven't got a choice, so get over it and good luck!

See you in the Free-From aisles,

Em xx

Dear Anyone Who Has Ever Been Affected By An Eating Disorder

With every other letter in this book I have had an idea of how it would go before I wrote it. I had a theme and points I wanted to make, and I knew whether it would be funny or sad or honest or ridiculous. I knew who I needed to talk to and how long it would take me to write. But with this one I didn't really know where to start because, if I'm honest with you, I didn't really know what to say. I've never really known what to say. I have seen countless friends sucked down this path, have had hundreds of conversations about it with dozens of people, and couldn't even count the amount of times I've spoken to worried parents who are having to watch their children's lives being taken over by an illness so severe that there is nothing they can do to stop it.

Each story is different – for every parent, every friend and every sufferer – but one thing that remains consistent through each of these conversations is the pain, the anguish and the heartbreak that all of those affected are feeling. Mothers who feel so hopeless, fathers who don't understand and, ultimately, those suffering, who just won't talk at all. Amongst the sadness, though, I have at times also felt so angry about all of this. Anger that an illness so seemingly *simple* is able to take full control over sensible, happy people's lives. Anger at how the answer to all of their problems seems so close, but is actually something they can't bring themselves to touch, and mostly I find myself so incredibly angry at some people's views of these issues.

I'm angry that people with anorexia are considered by some to be 'silly'. That people with bulimia are 'jokingly' deemed 'wasteful', and that people with binge-eating disorder are nothing more than 'greedy'. If you've never had to watch an eating disorder, never suffered with one or seen someone you love fighting one every day, you can't possibly understand the incredibly real and serious issue it is. You can't understand that when an eating disorder walks into a family, it becomes *everything*. It mercilessly tears lives and families apart and, as a result, you will never understand an eating disorder.

But this letter is not to those people. This is a letter for people who are being affected by eating disorders, who do know that families go through hell and who do understand the heartbreak. This letter is for people in the throes of these illnesses, to show you that things can and do get better. It is also for people currently watching one. I'm currently witnessing one of my closest friends battling every day to help her little sister. I don't want to talk too much about it, as it's not my story to share, but I want this to be dedicated to them.

My friend is one of the strongest and kindest people I know and watching her being so totally torn apart by the effect this disease is having on her sister has killed me to see. I love them both so much and I hope there will be a light at the end of the tunnel for them, as I do for the many people who are in need of help right now. I hope this letter reaches those who really need it, and that it helps them to realise that, if nothing else, they are not alone.

Like I say, I really didn't know *how* I was going to write this letter. So I did what every one of my generation does and turned to social media. I asked my Facebook friends if any of them who had suffered with an eating disorder would be willing to talk about it with me and share their stories. The response was overwhelming. Within the first five minutes I had floods of messages, all from people who were ready to talk: 'I don't mind you publishing it as it's designed to help others', 'I recovered last year so feel pretty strongly about helping others', 'Happy to share my story if it will help'. They went on and on and kept coming in, from people who were BETTER, who wanted to help. Who wanted to share their story, and who were ready to open up if it meant that one person who was still struggling would benefit.

And that's when I realised what this letter needed to be – it needed to be their stories. This story needed to be *them*. So here you go; here are the stories of my brave friends who have come together to help you, to help anyone who is currently, or watching someone they love, in the throes of an eating disorder.

(I have changed all of my friends' names to respect their privacy.)

Tom got in touch with me first, which surprised me, as it never occurred to me in the whole time I've known him that food, or his weight, had ever been an issue for him but, as he points out, this, '. . . so often happens; those of us who struggle seem the most confident externally'. Although he only sent me a short account of his story, I wanted to share it first because I think it's important we recognise that eating disorders do not only affect women.

He said: 'I've had various anxiety problems throughout my life. I was about ten when I started to monitor everything I ate. I starting running a lot and doing thousands of sit-ups a day.' At his worst he said he was eating about 500 calories a day.

'The problems came and went, but when I was fifteen I was diagnosed with anorexia and episodes of bulimia. I think I realised I had a serious problem when it became a point of contention at social events. I wouldn't eat a friend's birthday cake and, if I was made to do it, I would exercise afterwards to 'make up' for my indiscretion. To this day I have broad anxieties but still struggle with my body image, self-confidence and 'yo-yo' dieting. I think a salient detail is also the fact that only those closest to me have any idea this is the case.'

The next friend to get in touch was a girl I've known for years and years and years – both before, during and since her illness – who is now on the other side of a long battle with anorexia and living in London, working in a job she loves:

So, I'm writing this after a particularly happy session with my therapist – the man who first met me as an utterly crushed young girl, six or seven years ago – so I'm very much looking back with full awareness of how lucky I am to be so happy. (I also have wine and Quality Streets inside me, so this is a tiny bit of a rant . . .)

Two things that anger me (of many, by the way)

1. The perception that an eating disorder is an 'affectation' – an attention-seeking, selfish choice. Someone once told me that when I first became obviously ill, when it became a 'thing', a girl in the year above me had said, in a very casual, off-hand manner, 'Oh, so Harriet's decided to go anorexic'. As if this was ever my decision; as if, at age fourteen/ fifteen I had decided to project upon myself a severe mental illness that would rob me of my young, formative years. Even those I love most and who supported me most, didn't understand (in moments of desperation mostly) that it wasn't something I was 'choosing' to manifest. I never wanted everyone around me to have to live in my little world, dictated by the greedy, aggressive, nasty voices in my head. I felt guilty for years and sometimes, more rarely nowadays though, felt like I had to apologise for the pain I put people through. But it wasn't me, and it wasn't a choice, it was a serious illness. Certainly not some twisted extension of my desperate psyche craving attention.

2. Competitiveness. Now this is something that's really ugly, and something I've always been afraid to say, but people, subconsciously or not, pit people with eating disorders against one another. Someone else is

thinner, so you can't possibly be as ill as them. And to pardon the pun, that just feeds the self-hating voice in your head that tells you, that along with being a terrible, horrible person, you're also managing to be a failure at being thin and anorexic and ill. 'God, you're pathetic.' That's the voice talking, by the way. So please, I beg of you, don't ever compare people's stories. You wouldn't do it with any other serious illness, so what the hell gives you the right to do so to me?

And as an extra aside: it's an illness, an incredibly serious illness with terrifyingly high mortality rates in young women. That's tragic. Don't patronise, judge or measure a person's illness. Food is a manifestation of a chemical imbalance in the brain. Don't diminish the pain that someone goes through every moment of every day and night. They're already making themselves feel a hundred times worse than you ever could.

Things I've Learned

Therapy: If I were in charge for a day, I would make it so that therapy and regular therapy with no cut-off point were available for all who needed and/or wanted it. I am a lucky fuck. My mum worked her arse off for many years so, at my ultimate rock bottom (when school had asked me to leave, I saw no future and was tired of the constant self-loathing and doubt), she was able to get me onto a junior psychiatric ward within two weeks. Ninety-nine point nine per cent of eating disorder sufferers aren't like me. Therapy is the saviour, the safe place. And you also know you're starting to get better when you stage a coup at the aforementioned psychiatric ward when they try to cut off your internet access. What an infringement of basic human rights for a seventeen-year-old who desperately needed out, am I right? And probably distraction from the horrible sounds you hear down the corridor from the cries of a thirty-something woman being force-fed.

Drugs: Antidepressants alone aren't the answer but, you know what? You have a chemical imbalance in your brain. The classic analogy is insulin: if you were diabetic you wouldn't have to be ashamed of your reliance on daily medication. I've made my peace with the fact that I will probably not stop taking the little green and yellow pill (Prozac) every morning for many years. I'm OK with it and, what's more, I'm grateful. It keeps the voice at bay. And that's what my eating disorder was/is: a physical release of the unbearable pressure of that voice in my mind.

Exercise: Exercise, although only when healthy enough to do so, saved my sanity. Sweat, loud music, and making your muscles do things you never thought they could when they were all wasted away is the most life-affirming feeling in the world.

To end on a positive note

I'm still pissed, and I'm still bitter. School didn't support me, some hospital staff were downright horrible (even with the benefit of hindsight) and I will never get those formative years back. In some ways I'm older than I should be, and in some I'm much younger than I should feel.

But I'm on the other side and I'm so grateful. The friends who stood by me not only made me own up to my selfish actions, they also defended me to others and loved and supported me beyond imagination. The unexpected people who gave me moments of such kindness still bring a tear to my eye. When I returned to school after a term out, the friend of a friend who whispered in my ear on my first day that it was so good to see me back – moments like that make me happier than any sad times I remember.

I'm not happy for those horrible, dark and lonely years in my life but they taught me one of the most important things I've learned, and something I really try to live by: that life is for the living, everyone deserves to be happy, and only you can really make yourself happy.'

The next message came from a girl I've known for about six years, and in that time I never knew she had a problem until she got in touch with me about this chapter. Francesca struggled with bulimia and this is her story:

This is how it started: I was about thirteen. I went to a very small village primary school with less than 100 students. Throughout primary school I was very confident and I'd never hesitate to express my ideas in class. I didn't ever worry if someone wanted to speak to me or not and I certainly never thought about my weight. Yes, I was aware that I was quite short and my hair wasn't as nice as some of the other girls, but I never thought about my size (and, to be fair, I was a very healthy weight pre-teens).

It was a big jump to secondary school; suddenly there were three times as many people in my form alone than there had been in my whole year at primary school. This didn't faze me too much; a couple of the boys from my year were also in my form, so I wasn't alone. But then they suddenly didn't want to be my friend anymore. I made friends with a new group of people and that was OK. But I never felt truly comfortable around them. They had all come from the same primary school and lived close together, whereas I would have to travel for about an hour to see them outside school. They would make fun of me a lot and there was a constant nagging voice at the back of my mind that they didn't really like me at all. That nagging voice was where the anxiety started, and it grew.

Looking back, it seems that I was some sort of scapegoat. And to this day I have no idea if we were actually friends or not. Maybe it was just my insecurities getting the best of me and it really was 'all in my head'. But either way, to be feeling that level of discomfort and anxiety – not just around your friends, but actively caused by them – isn't a healthy environment to be in.

I turned to food and books to occupy my mind and distract me from the sick feeling at the bottom of my stomach. I kid you not, I would munch my way through multipacks of sausage rolls and pots of Pringles, holed up in my bedroom with my head in a book. My parents didn't know that I would sneak off and buy them as I walked to meet my nanny after my clarinet lesson.

It took a while, but suddenly the impact of what I was doing hit me. Looking at a photo, I realised I had ballooned. I felt sick with myself. How had I not noticed this happening? How could I undo it? I vowed to stop comfort eating. No more cakes or pizza from the school canteen and definitely no more sausage rolls and Pringles.

Unfortunately my realisation only led to further anxiety – now I had my weight to feel insecure about too. It wasn't long before I turned to food again to comfort myself. Only this time, instead of not thinking anything of it, I felt sick with myself afterwards. So, so sick. What had I done? And I knew I had to get the food out of me right there and then. So I knelt down in front of the toilet and stuck two fingers down my throat.

It wasn't as easy as I thought it would be. I heaved but nothing except bile came up. I pushed my fingers further and further down my throat, wiggling them about, tears streaming down my face. Eventually it came. It was horrible, like a roaring wave, coming again and again. As I caught my breath, I vowed to not put myself through this again. I never wanted to feel like this again.

When I realised it was a problem

I think I knew deep down that what I was doing wasn't healthy. Not just physically (fortunately my teeth are absolutely fine, but that's not always the way with bulimics) but mentally too. For me, it turned into a way in which I could be in control. I might not be able to control the burning anxiety within me, I might not be able to stop myself binge eating, but at least I could get it out of myself afterwards. I knew it was bad, but I didn't know how to stop.

I wasn't a consistent bulimic. I would go through phases of not doing it, but it would always creep back into my life. I also went through phases of limiting my food intake to a dangerously low amount (though these phases never lasted long, as I really love food).

It wasn't all about binge eating with a book all the time; when I went to university and was in control of my own diet I simply made the wrong food choices, and alcohol definitely didn't help.

My weight went up and down a lot throughout my teens. Aged thirteen I was quite large, by sixteen I was an average weight again, and then I hit my heaviest aged nineteen. Again I saw a picture of myself and my stomach dropped. That was when I realised I needed to make a change. I stepped on the scales, then worked out my BMI, and I was horrified. I was dangerously close to the obese end of the scale. I think it took seeing those statistics in writing that made me realise I needed to change my lifestyle.

How I dealt with it/recovery

I started by simply trying to eat a bit healthier, but I'd never really been educated about it so I really struggled. A friend suggested I tried using an app called MyFitnessPal, which is essentially a calorie counter, but it also shows you your macros, so you can see how balanced your diet is.

This was an absolute game-changer. I set a goal and I knew as long as I stuck to it I would be getting better. It helped to stop me from bingeing because I would have to record it and then see that I'd let myself down that day. And even if I made myself sick afterwards, there was no way of recording that. It didn't magically cure me, I did slip up a few times, but it acted as an extra barrier that helped me binge and purge less and less.

I lost ten kilograms (one-and-a-half stone) in six months. Then another half a stone over the next six months. I felt fantastic. But then my final university exams came and I was so stressed I couldn't sleep and couldn't eat. If I did manage to eat, I could rarely manage to keep it down (through no fault of my own this time). Fortunately I got through my exams and things went back to normal and I got back on track. But I do still find that my appetite dissipates during periods of stress now, rather than turning to comfort eating like I used to.

While using an app like MyFitnessPal helped me control myself more and helped me lose weight, running has absolutely been the best thing for helping me with my wellbeing. Not only does it make me feel a lot more relaxed about my diet, but it also helps me relieve stress, separate work time from home time, and I always have a new challenge to be working towards.

At the start of 2016 I couldn't run for more than about two minutes without starting to struggle, and now I've signed up for my first 10k. Nothing has been more helpful to the girl who used to dread getting changed in P.E. and having to run 400m for athletics season. Teaching myself to run is something I have done entirely by myself, for myself.

The last story was from someone I had known only in the latter stages of her recovery, but who was adamant that despite the fact she hardly knew me at all, she wanted to help in any way she could. Kristina is now twenty-four and has been battling the illness for the last eight years.

At the age of sixteen I decided to go on a diet. I had always been quite chubby and I just wanted to lose a bit of weight. Like most girls, I wanted to be able to go to Topshop, buy whatever I wanted and look great in it. It began with cutting out chocolate, sweets and crisps – anything you would usually avoid on a diet. I inevitably lost some weight and was receiving positive comments from friends and family, and even teachers at my school were saying I looked great! I then decided to up my game and cut out carbs, thinking the positive comments would increase. The comments kept coming, and I was feeling great getting all this attention. So then, before I knew it, it was goodbye to dairy and then protein. In no time at all it had got to the stage where I was eating only vegetables. I went down four dress sizes in about five months, and the strange thing was I didn't even feel that tired. I think I was high on losing weight.

As I was at a boarding school, I was able to hide most of this from my parents, but from my friends? Not so much. They were quick to notice and soon informed teachers they were worried about me. Unbelievably, however, my best friend was actually told she was just suffering with severe jealousy as I was getting more attention from the boys. But they didn't give up. One friend, who had previously been anorexic, told her mum, who then got in touch with my mum.

The next thing I knew my mum was at my school, in my room, begging me to admit I had a problem. She was so upset telling me that she saw the signs but just didn't know what to do. At first I denied it all, but thinking about it I began to realise that I actually, honestly, felt too scared to eat. I was addicted. Addicted to losing weight. Addicted to restricting calories. Addicted to the sense of control I felt.

I was then taken to a GP. They took my weight and my stats and, although my weight and BMI weren't dangerously low at that point, my blood pressure and heart rate were. In the next blink I found myself in a children's ward at The Priory. I was there just for a short time, about six weeks. My consultant thought they could nip it in the bud, (i.e. feed me and then I'd be fine). I really wanted this to be true. I cried every day wanting to be home or with my friends – my friends who, by the way, never failed to amaze me with their support.

To be honest, physically, yes, The Priory helped me, but mentally, day by day, I was getting sicker. I left that ward after a short time and returned to school but was back again just a few months later. I had lost even more weight. I was there for about ten weeks that time. I then left, lost more weight, and was back again about ten months later. I felt so bad; I didn't want to hurt my family or my friends, but I kept screwing up. Something inside me was making me restrict what I ate.

My friends and family at this time were my rock. My friends called and visited me, which, considering we were all eighteen, couldn't have been easy. My mum had always been understanding but it was my dad who really struggled. There were times when he would beg me to JUST EAT. I would cry and tell him I JUST COULDN'T. But soon he began to read so many books. He even enrolled on a training course about anorexia that King's College was running, in order to better understand what I was going through. I don't tell him this enough, but the support I got from him then was truly amazing.

Despite this, however, things still weren't easy; my weight was dropping and I was going to extreme lengths to hide food I was meant to eat, which I am now so mortified about! (I am not going to discuss the things

I did, as I don't want this story to be triggering or providing tips for anyone struggling.)

In 2011 I started university. Doctors were unsure but I was adamant I was going to go. I was there for eight weeks. I made amazing friends, had so much fun, but I just couldn't eat. I was told by a doctor that I couldn't carry on like this but I realised I couldn't change. It took all my strength but I had to admit I couldn't cope. A month later I was in an NHS ward in Tottenham, for what was probably the worst six months of my life. I wasn't allowed to leave my room for five days at a time. I wasn't allowed to go outside. I had a nurse who was with me the whole time, even when I went to the toilet or showered. BUT my friends and family never failed to amaze me. My parents, who are based in north Essex, always went to the parent support meetings. My friends would visit whenever they could. This support literally saw me through!

I then left and went on an amazing holiday and started university again the following September. My BMI was still low but I saw a team and my GP once or twice a week. And I had so much fun it was unreal! The first year flew past. It was all going so well, but then in the last weekend of November, during my second year, I broke my femur. I had been told previously that I had severe osteoporosis as a result of my weight loss, but it hadn't really registered. Next thing I knew, after falling up some stairs as I was tipsy, I had smashed to pieces the biggest bone in my body. I was rushed to hospital and was there for over a week. Again my family and friends were by my side.

I then went home and attended a day centre for people with eating disorders, determined after that shock that I wanted to get better, but unfortunately I was triggered by everyone there. There was huge competition to be the 'best anorexic' and I wanted to succeed. My parents had no idea that I was lying when I told them it was helping me.

The next thing I knew it was September again, and I was being told I had to go to hospital or I would be sectioned. I had been planning to go back to university for my last year to a house with my friends, so I was in shock; I cried and refused. But I had no choice – it was going voluntarily or being sectioned. So I went. I cried so much, for so long. But yet again my family and friends always came to see me. My parents were there at least twice a week and I had one friend who would come at least once every seven days. I was in hospital for a year. It was the worst, yet best thing that ever happened to me. I actually felt I was getting better, something I never thought would happen.

For me, my recovery started after a holiday. A few months before I left hospital I was allowed to go to Rome with friends for a long weekend. I made the decision before I went that I wanted to be 'normal'. I was drinking wine, eating pasta and enjoying life. It wasn't easy, and the guilt was unreal, but I did it and had the best trip ever. This was the catalyst for my recovery. A few months

later, I went away to Greece with my family and this was
the best holiday we'd had in seven years, as there were
no arguments about food or me freaking out at dinner.
I realised life was so much better without this horrible
illness. I was then discharged in September and went for
a weekend away to Prague with my friend where, again,
we drank beer (as it was cheaper than water!), ate amazing
food, laughed so much and stayed out until 5 a.m.

I started university again and had the best two
housemates I could have wished for. I was extremely close
to one of them and she was my absolute rock. Then a
close friend on my course watched as her brother became
sick with leukaemia. For me that was a huge turning
point. I saw her crying and in so much pain and I realised
that I didn't want to be doing that to my family and
friends anymore. I was doing well at the time but was
often toying with the idea of succumbing once more to
anorexia but, after this, I realised I didn't want to.

I was having fun; I was going out and properly
socialising. I was doing well at university, as I wasn't
constantly thinking about what I would eat later. I was
enjoying life! I never thought I would recover, but I did.
And I honestly feel that happened because of all the love
and support I got from friends and family. They all went
above and beyond. My family always went to meetings,
read books, and went to family sessions to try to help and,
very importantly, to understand me. My friends? Well,
they never left my side. In hospital they would call, visit
me (although it was a trek!) and send me presents. Once

more they gave me strength. I was never left out and knew they all just wanted me to recover. Even now they are so protective and so understanding. Recovery is NOT EASY, but it's so worthwhile. If you're struggling, please speak to a friend, a parent or a professional to get some support.

Just remember, we are strong enough to get anorexic so we are strong enough to recover!

So there are some stories from some of my incredibly brave friends. I will never be able to thank them enough for being so honest with me and sharing their experiences, nor will I be able to tell them how proud of them I am for their recovery. I hope, I really do, that their honesty has helped you in some way, whether you are currently suffering with an eating disorder or if you are witnessing someone you love being consumed by one. Disordered eating is an affliction that affects SO many of us, and it is still something we don't know enough about or talk enough about. I want to see that change.

I hope by sharing their stories my friends are able to inspire you in some capacity and that, if you do feel you are in need of help, that you feel strong enough to reach out for it. There will always be someone there for you, you must remember that. If you don't feel ready to talk to friends or family about it, you can get in touch with B-EAT, the UK's eating disorder charity, on these numbers:

Adult Helpline: 0345 634 1414 or email help@b-eat.co.uk.
Youthline: 0345 634 7650 or email fyp@b-eat.co.uk.

Please remember that you are stronger than you know, and I'm always here for you.

All my love,

Em xxxx

Dear Boys

Initially I was disinclined to write this letter as I deemed it quite unnecessary, but something inside me told me it might be worth doing. A lot of the time I actually consider gender to be irrelevant – what can boys *really* do better than girls, right? But then I had a think back to some of the most painstakingly awful moments of my teenage years and realised that many of them had come about as a result of the boys in my life not understanding me, or what I was going through, at all. So I've put together a little guide for you – nothing groundbreaking, but something I hope you will find helpful. You can thank me later.

To any woman who has accidentally picked up this letter, I ought to say this: I am not trying to be all sexist and generalised and paint all females with the same brush. Please don't freak out about that. I know we are all different. These are coming from me, one woman, who at one point or another in her life, has wanted to say this to a man. You may well want to say something totally different, and that is of course OK.

Once a month we have periods
I know you know this, but let me explain them to you in a little more detail.

- Blood does not continually fall out of us the entire time we're on our period.
- We do NOT appreciate it when you describe it as any of the following: being on the blob, a shark attack, Dracula's tea bag, the curse, having the painters and decorators in, being on the rag, riding the crimson wave, ripping the Japanese Flag or birthing a blood diamond.
- Tampons are only 'disgusting' once they've been used.
- PMS is a legit thing and NO, you don't get it in sympathy.
- It does drastically alter our mood.
- It doesn't make our vaginas hurt.
- It does make our stomachs hurt.
- It causes bloating.
- No, we did not deliberately get it two days into our summer holiday.
- It does not mean that you are entitled to blowjobs all week.
- A period can last from two to seven days.
- Occasionally they provide moments of sweet, sweet relief when we realise that we are not carrying your child.
- They make us so tired.
- Yes, we really do crave chocolate when we have it.
- It makes our boobs hurt, and occasionally it makes them itch.
- On average we will use 11,000 tampons in our lives,

so please refrain from freaking out every time you find one in our bags.

- It is messy, but period sex is totally fine.
- Sometimes it will leak and we will stain the sheets. This is not our fault, nor is it a big deal.
- Same story with our pants. Do you think we wanted to ruin our favourite pair of Agent Provocateur knickers by bleeding into them? No, we didn't. So please refrain from freaking out.
- It can cause some of the biggest spots that you have ever seen.
- Periods do not attract bears.
- Periods do not attract vampires.
- Periods do not attract sharks.

Sometimes we get emotional and we're not entirely sure why

We are literally chock-a-block full of hormones and sometimes it takes nothing more than seeing a baby duckling on the side of the road to set us off. This doesn't mean we are volatile, or crazy, or a nightmare. It just means that, for some reason, oestrogen is on double time and everything becomes incredibly upsetting. It's not necessarily your fault, but if you ask me one more time why I'm 'being so crazy', then you ought to know that it won't necessarily be my fault when I punch you in the throat. We don't like feeling like this as much as you don't like witnessing it, so why not go ahead and make it easier for us by just backing up about five feet and shutting the hell up. Until we need hugs and positive affirmations that is; then you must return, in the least irritating way possible.

When we say our boobs hurt it's because they actually hurt, and not just because we don't want to have sex with you

Sometimes our tits hurt and we don't know why. Probably as a result of that pesky oestrogen again. It's nothing personal, and it's not code for 'hands off my knockers, I know where this is going and I'm tired so this isn't going to happen'. If we wear an unsupportive bra while walking a long way, doing lots of stairs or on a run, they will hurt. They also get tender at that time of the month and when they are growing. There are lots of reasons so, rather than being a dick about it, why not be sympathetic?

We have just as much weird hair as you

You're covered in the stuff, so when mysterious little strands appear in new places you either won't notice or it will be unsurprising. But for a girl, finding a long black hair on her chin can be frightening and very surprising. IT IS NORMAL. Don't freak out. That doesn't mean that you're dating a man, or that your friend is secretly a werewolf. Women get hairs coming out of moles, hair in their nose, moustaches, hairy arms, hairy toes and face hair JUST LIKE YOU. We don't complain about it on your body, so why not repay us the favour, eh?

Body hair removal – the truth

It costs approximately £40 to get a bikini wax in London and it hurts like buggery, so you'll forgive us if we're not rushing to the salon every six weeks. Here are some other facts about body hair you'd do well to learn:

- In between waxes we have to wait for it to grow back, so that means it'll be itchy and untidy for a few weeks.
- Same story with our legs.
- If we shave our underarms every day it's a stubbly nightmare; sometimes we have to leave it for a couple.
- It is natural.
- It is not disgusting.
- We will deal with it but we either can't be arsed or are waiting for something, so don't whatever you do ask about it.
- Epilating really hurts and you are forbidden from commenting until you've had a go at it. (Before you scoff and say you would do it easily you probably ought to know that an epilator pulls that hair out of your skin one by one, like lots of little tweezers on acid.)
- It's not uncommon for a girl to get her moustache waxed or threaded.
- Yes, our eyebrow maintenance IS that important, so back off.
- If we don't want to remove various parts of our body hair it is not your job to tell us to. At the end of the day, our beauty regime is our decision. So just like we don't expect you to trim your pubes and shave your

legs, might we please ask that we are rewarded with
the same courtesy? If we want pubic hair growing
every which way and you have a problem with that,
then you're an arsehole. No, it may not be the most
aesthetically pleasing thing you've ever seen, but it's
attached to a woman who has every right to grow her
pubes down to her knees and curl them into beautiful
ringlets if she so wishes, so respect that.

Queefing is NOT the end of the world

Sometimes this happens and we don't fully know why. Just
go with it, it's not disgusting; it's simply air being forced out
of the vagina. In fact, it's actually pretty funny. Gauge the
room, but if it seems appropriate then laugh – it will help to
ease the embarrassment of the woman it has just come out of.
She didn't do it on purpose and will probably be mortified,
although God knows why because it's something totally out
of our control.

We do need to be told that we don't look fat in that. AGAIN

We are not asking you because we want the truth. We are
asking you because we really need a confidence boost. Don't
roll your eyes and, if the truth is going to hurt, probably best
not to say it. DEFINITELY best not to say it if you're already
running late to a party and you're onto the one hundredth
outfit of the night and tears could be imminent. We know
it's mad and irrational to keep asking but we can't help it.

Girl fights are different to boy fights

God I wish they weren't, but they are. We don't fix things
with a quick brawl in the street and then a beer back at
the bar. We talk in code, via WhatsApp normally and
confrontation is avoided at all costs. Yes, we KNOW that she
is our best friend of ten years and that it's silly to fight over
something so small, but we can't help it, this is instrumental
to the growth of our friendship and ultimately one of those
things that just happens. Let us be little bitches; no, it's not
our colour, we're not proud of it, but it'll probably all be OK
in the end. Either be on our side or get the bloody hell out.

Vaginas don't really smell that bad

Stop going round and asking people to smell your 'fishy
fingers'. Our vaginas don't really smell like that and you are
being a vulgar little prick. Each vagina has its own smell
and most of them really don't smell that strong or that badly
anyway. If they do, it's often the sign of a problem and NOT
something you should be pointing out.

Vaginas are self-cleaning

Just telling you that because it's pretty cool.

We poo too

Everyone poos and it's incredibly annoying that we are
made to feel that we shouldn't. You stride into the bog with
a newspaper and a cup of coffee, making a right spectacle
of the whole thing before taking a photo of it, showing me
and my parents and sharing it on ratemypoo.com and we're

expected to wait until you've gone to sleep before we sneak in there for a plopless shit? Yeah, no, I don't think so.

Girls masturbate

Probably not with foot-long dildos like you see in the films and perhaps not as often or with as much vigour as you, but we do do it and we don't necessarily like talking about it that much, so let's stop asking about it at inappropriate times like in the classroom or at a dinner party.

We won't look like the porn stars

Never will I'm afraid. In real life we won't all be clean-shaven, flat-stomached and winking at you with enormous eyes when we suck your willies. Don't expect too much.

We're not all the same

All this 'girls like cuddles', 'girls like flowers', 'girls dream of big weddings' shit drives me mad. Some of us do like cuddles and flowers and want big weddings; some of us hate people in our personal space, have terrible pollen allergies and plan on dying alone. Stop stereotyping us all with the princess brush, eh? Each woman wants different things, so best to get to know a person before making assumptions.

We don't like being leered at from moving cars

This is NOT a compliment. Being harassed on the street is never ever a nice experience. You might think you're being friendly, that you are showing your appreciation, but you're not. You're making us uncomfortable and we would rather you stopped. We didn't get all dressed up for you, and just because we've got a skirt on or there's a bit of cleavage out does not stand as an invitation to stare or comment. They are our bodies and our choices and you would do well to remember this. If this is still proving tricky, why not imagine that the woman your friends are leering at and commenting on is your sister. All of a sudden it stops becoming harmless banter and you will probably be overwhelmed with the temptation to beat them up. That's how that girl's brother feels.

The job of contraception is not exclusively ours

Don't expect all women to be on the pill or have the coil fitted, or assume that because you like going in bareback that she's going to be OK with that. We don't know where you've been and the least you can do is offer some respect to a woman who's letting you into her bed. Couple that with the fact that we can't just walk away from pregnancies, should they occur, I think it's fair to say that if you think you're going to get lucky it is your responsibility to not only bring a condom but wear it, whether you particularly want to or not.

And here are a few more little notes for the total cavemen amongst you:

- Our place is NOT in the kitchen.
- We are not a 'slag' if we enjoy and/or have a lot of sex.
- We are just as capable at pretty much everything.

- Tits were not put on our body to be stared at. They were actually put there to feed our children with.
- Treating a girl 'mean' won't keep her keen.
- Women who love other women (lesbians) are not doing it for your enjoyment or sexual pleasure.
- We have made the decision to either put on make-up, or not, because it makes US feel good and has nothing to do with you.
- While we often appreciate chivalry, our world won't end if we find ourselves in a situation where we have to get our hair wet or carry our own bags. We do manage fine on our own all the times that we're not with you.
- Our feet do stink.
- We fart and are not totally against blaming it on the dog.

That probably isn't even close to everything; in fact, I know it's not. But there is so much to know. Basically it boils down to this: we are the same species but different breeds. If you wouldn't like it done to you, chances are we don't want it done to us. Respect is key. As long as you can respect a woman then you can't go too far wrong.

Good luck!

Em xx

Dear Equalists Of The Future

Now before I start, I need to say this: I am a feminist, of course I am. I see absolutely no reason why there shouldn't be absolute equality of the sexes. As a child I wanted to be Secretary General of the United Nations and I saw no reason why my gender would ever get in the way of that; it didn't even occur to me that it might. I have never needed or even thought that I needed a man to define myself. And I am the sister of the girl who wanted nothing more than to go to Eton School, not understanding how it was possibly fair that this school was considered the best in the country, where they were taught to build cars, but that it wasn't an option for her simply because she had a vagina. My friends are all feminists, my family are all feminists, my boyfriend is a feminist – in that they all categorically believe there should be equality of the sexes. As it should be.

But if we're honest, and we're going to need to be, 'feminism' has become a dirty word. You see, in a poll done by the *Huffington Post* in 2014, 82 per cent of respondents said they believed 'men and women should be social, political and economic equals' (the definition of feminism) but only 20 per cent identified as feminists. Which says to me that although they ALL want what feminism should stand for, there's a reason people are recoiling away from the movement as if it were a Tinder date who's just told them they're riddled with crabs. And I think I know what that reason is. But first things first, let's go back to that statistic. We know that 18 per cent of respondents don't believe we should be equal (and to my mind should be given a good hard clip around the ears for that), and that the remaining 82 per cent believe there should be total equality of the sexes, but when asked to brand themselves with the f-tag, 62 per cent of them are dropping off.

Is it because they don't know the definition of feminism and believe that in order to be one they have to eschew the razor, buy lots of cats, be prepared to get very political on Facebook and banish all men, and they don't want to do that because they take pride in their appearance, don't care for long ranty Facebook posts, are in a long-term relationship and fucking hate cats? Are they doing it because they're men and think feminism is a job for women? That it's a tag that removes their masculinity? Or is actually because there are now so many connotations attached to the word feminism that they don't want to associate with it?

I have this terrible feeling it's the latter. When the idea for this book was just a tiny seed, I spent a lot of time talking to a lot of people about feminism as a whole and was saddened but not entirely surprised when, in answer to the question, 'What's the first thing that comes to mind when you think of a feminist?', the words 'hairy', 'scary', 'angry' and 'bitter' were said long before 'strong', 'empowering' 'inspirational' or 'equality'. In fact, the bad words outranked the good ones about ten to one with terms like 'lesbian', 'sandals', 'self-righteous', 'man-hating', 'aggressive' and 'big' being the most common. And I'm not proud to admit it, but I *get* why there are these connotations, why people don't want to brand themselves with the 'f-word'. I don't *like* it, but I do get it.

Because you know what? Even though I consider myself a strong feminist, one that would fight every day for the rest of my life for gender equality, I ought to admit that there are times when I do feel scared – is that the right word? – of other feminists. No, not scared exactly, but certainly inferior. I don't know when it happened, or actually why it has happened, but the whole concept has become so exclusive. It's like if you don't bother identifying as 'feminist as fuck' in your Twitter bio then you needn't bother applying. If you don't share only black-and-white images of yourself wearing 'I HAVE A VAGINA' T-shirts or dedicate your Instagram feed exclusively to women with long underarm hair, then you're just not *in*.

In fact, I'm friends with a girl on Facebook who became the inspiration for this whole letter after she posted a status last year that made my blood boil, and in one sentence gave me enough inspiration for an entire book. She claimed that, as a girl of mixed-race heritage, she was 'sick of all these white middle-class women identifying as feminists' and that, as a result of the influx of them to the feminist movement, she was going to stop identifying as such. Maybe she said this because she felt they were diluting the brand; maybe she said it because she feels that white middle-class women aren't *cool* enough, or she thinks that, for whatever reason, they are immune from sexism. Or maybe she feels these women have chosen a life of nothing more than attending the office parties of their husbands once every couple of months as a sweet break from cleaning up after their adorable Middletonesque children day in day out – so as a result they must lie in the bed they've made. Either way, this is a woman who has dedicated her entire life to fighting for gender equality. She is one of the aforementioned 'feminist as fuck' slogan-ed, T-shirt-wearing, hairy armpit-photo-sharing types. So what the fuck is she playing at?

As a white woman – a white, southwest London-residing, feminist woman, no less – I all of a sudden felt incredibly targeted. Like I wasn't important to the movement. Like I was annoying. Like I was hindering it in some way. But what the likes of this girl don't seem to understand is that that's impossible. It's impossible that ANYONE identifying as a feminist can POSSIBLY be a bad thing, because that's the whole point! It's equality. It's more people fighting for equality. It's one more person in the ranks. It's bringing us another step closer to what we are fighting for. Or did I miss something while I was busy believing that together we could fight for a better world? While I wasn't looking did it become a members' club saved only for those who have actually and physically burned their bras while marching on Trafalgar Square and had the black-and-white photos of them doing it banned under Instagram's nudity rules, which they've then contested as FREEDOM OF EXPRESSION? If so, tell me right now. I'm sorry, but as long as people

are *scared* of feminists – as long as other women who are
TRYING to make a difference are *scared of them* – then
the whole feminist movement has been rendered irrelevant
anyway, because by pushing away the very people we need
to move it forwards, it stops being a movement altogether
and just becomes a static. Which is no fucking good to
anyone.

Ladies. Gents. FEMINISTS. I think it's time for some
damage control. If we are going to make this work, if
we are going to keep it moving (which we do NEED
to do), then we are going to have to go right back to
the drawing board. We are going to need to re-establish
the END result and get over ourselves to the point of
understanding that men are not the enemy, that we can
utilise the ones willing to identify as a feminist, and
ultimately stop focusing all our attention on who we
have fighting our corner and what their marital status
might be, whether or not celebrities are doing enough
to be deemed worthy of the feminist title, and turn our
attention to those that really need it: the individuals
needing our help. The women who aren't getting paid as
much as their male co-workers, despite doing exactly the
same job. The ones not being considered for jobs simply
because they've reached an age where maternity leave
might be on the cards. The ones who have been victims
of sexual assault and are afraid to speak up. The ones who
are being objectified, either at the workplace or on the
streets. The ones who are victims of domestic abuse. The
ones both here and abroad who are being subjected to

female genital mutilation. Those girls who are being sold into the sex industry, or being forced to be child brides. Girls that are having to leave school because they've started their periods and are made to feel frightened and ashamed of it. Women everywhere who are being deprived of the same opportunities as their male counterparts simply because of their sex. There is a fuck-ton of shit to get done if we stand a chance at an equal world, but none of this is going to change if the very matriarchs holding this entire movement together are pointing fingers and getting choosy. Don't you see that to make this change, whether you like it or not, we are going to NEED to work together?

There is overwhelming evidence to suggest that the feminist movement is working wonders, and right now women are doing better than at any point in history. We are business owners, famous authors, CEOs, world leaders, billionaires. We're successful. Gone are the days when women did nothing but wait at home for the menfolk to finish work with four babies to their (husband's last) name, a lasagne in the oven and their legs open. We are rocking the shit out of life right now. Social media is just brimming with #girlbosses; we're single mothers, working mothers, hard-working badass bitches.

So why is it that, despite the fact we are seemingly stronger and more successful than we've ever been, that insecurities, depression, anxiety and eating disorders are at an all-time high? Have we, as feminists, got to the point where we're so consumed with getting a woman into the workplace that we neglect to care that she's crying into her Cheerios before she gets on the tube in the morning? And ultimately, importantly, I have to ask, is there a connection between the overwhelming 'success' of feminism and the crippling unhappiness of women? To a degree, I worry there is.

Feminist readers, hopefully all of you, take this moment to place the book down, take hold of your hair and yank it while calling me every curse word under the sun and, once that's out of your system, I will continue.

You see, for years we blamed the unhappiness of women on society, and rightly so; society fucked us royally. Laws weren't in our favour, adverts were downright sexist and jobs didn't exist. The rules we lived by were ones dreamed up by the men in power – our MPs, bosses, husbands. Our society. But what do we do now? Who can we blame? Society is still fucking us up, it's still saying we need to be a certain size, telling us where to breastfeed our children, ordering us not to eat certain things, judging us on our figures, encouraging us to remove all of our body hair, making us feel ashamed of our decision to go back to work as promptly as possible after having babies. Society is still a bitch. But who do we blame when, after all this time, we make up a sizable chunk of it?

It's not OK, nor is it fair that we make up only 29 per cent of MPs, or that we are only 26 per cent of the House of Lords; nor is it OK that only 25.2 per cent of UK judges are women or that we account for only 17 per cent of UK business owners but, but . . . if you remove the 'only's from those facts, and compare them to where we were twenty years ago, there is definitely something to be celebrated. At least we're there. Look at the progress we've made. Every year I watch these percentages rise; every year more female MPs are voted in and more women become high court judges. And yet, at the same rate, statistics of mental health issues and bullying in schools and even obesity in women are also on the up. How can it be that the more successful we get the less happy we are? This goes against everything we have been taught to expect out of life, and everything we were promised in the fight for equality. This is the thing that's worrying me the most.

The fight for equal opportunity has been outstanding. I'm well aware that if it wasn't for my foremothers I wouldn't be sitting here, writing a book, aged twenty-three, in a world where it's totally acceptable not to have children or a husband. And it's going to continue to get better, how can it not? More and more women are ready to stand up. More and more men are ready to stand in our corner.

We were the first generation to have single mothers as the norm. As a result, we no longer need to prove ourselves. They know we can do it; they know we can do anything. The 'my missus needs to be able to do two things: suck my dick and make a sandwich' blokes of this world are a dying breed, or a bullshitting one at any rate, and I know with certainty that, thanks to women like Lena Dunham and Caitlin Moran, we are going to be fine. We are going to continue to thrive until one day we will make up at least 50 per cent of parliament, guaranteed.

Despite the internal feuding within the feminist movement that I've spent the last few pages whingeing about, there is no doubt in my mind that our hard work will be rewarded. That it will continue to grow and get better, that we will see victory after victory. Look at the success of the Women's March on Washington in January 2017 – the most remarkable feminist event in my lifetime so far. For that, for a really fucking important cause, all this stupid class shit was forgotten and we did what we had to do. All over the world men, women and children stood together to fight against a man, a president who will not fight and who has not fought for us, and I have never been prouder to be a woman. We marched as our foremothers did before us and we showed our children how to march too. We marched on Washington and we marched on London because we had to, and we marched so that one day we wouldn't have to. THAT was feminism at its most beautiful, at its best and its brightest. THAT is why I am a feminist and that is why I know with 100 per cent certainty that one day we will win, we will be equal.

But I need to know, how much collateral we can expect in the interim? Mental health issues are currently occurring in one out of four of us and I need more than my fingers and toes to count how many good friends have had to battle an eating disorder. If you haven't had a mental health issue at some point in your life, then you will certainly know someone who has. The world is rife with them. But why is this a feminist issue? Why am I bringing this up here and now? Men are affected by mental health issues, too. In fact,

suicide is much more prevalent in men and is actually the
biggest killer of men under the age of forty-five, outranking
death from cancer, diabetes and road accidents. Men don't
have it easy at all, and I'm not for a moment saying they do.
But right now I'm talking about women. About the fact that
women everywhere are unhappy, whether they're fighting
a mental illness, an eating disorder, or just struggling to
stay afloat. I'm talking about the fact that the pressure on
us is higher than it has ever been; that most of the Grade A
bitchiness I see on social media comes from women and is
meant for women; that words like 'ample assets' and 'pert
derrière' are used by women about women in national
newspapers; that women are slut-shamed, body-shamed,
hair-shamed, everything-shamed, all the time, by OTHER
women. Which, in a world where we are *supposed* to be
standing together, is just abhorrent.

I think the problem is this: there is just not enough
support stemming from the feminist movement.
Empowerment? Yes. Success? Yes. Support? No. At what
point are we going to look around and realise that, YES,
this fight for equality is essential, but that in order to
create the next generation of women willing to fight for
our cause, we are going to need to raise them to love
themselves and love each other first and foremost? As long
as we're trampling on each other's heads to get to the top,
forcing our views down each other's throats and deeming
someone 'too white', 'too posh' or 'too uneducated' to
fight the feminist movement, we're seriously not going
to get anywhere. There is no such thing as overcrowding

when it comes to feminism. The whole concept, the whole definition, was a cause made for a million and one. It was made up of roll–up–your–sleeves, pull–up–another–chair, can–do attitudes, and I'll be damned if I watch that slide now. There is no such thing as too many feminists.

Part of me thinks that 'feminism' shouldn't even be a word anymore. Although the concept is still as important now as it was at the beginning, it's the word that's become the problem. It's the connotations. The other day someone who will remain nameless was having a big old go at me (don't ask) and among some of the disgusting insults he threw my way a couple stuck out: 'You're a man–hating feminist'. It was so weird, having these words spat at me, totally out of the blue, as if they were the ugliest words in the world. The whole thing made me SO angry that the label which should mean 'world changer' was being thrown at me as if it was something to be ashamed of. My feminism is something I SHOULD feel incredibly proud of, but still, somehow, I was made to feel there was something wrong with it; like it was stupid, ugly, pointless. And, worryingly, I don't think this was even just the drunken ramblings of one stupid man. I think the fact this 'insult' even came to the surface during his rant says to me that on some subconscious level 'feminism' is a word that's kept in the insult bank.

Not so sure? Why not imagine yourself screaming 'YOU FUCKING ANIMAL–LOVING TWAT' mid–argument at someone who volunteers at the RSPCA and you might start to see what I mean. So what is going on here? I'm

not sure. But I do know that the fact this even happened
means that feminism is no longer screaming: 'GREAT
PIONEERING MOVEMENT' as it should but has instead
turned into something a lot of people, just below the surface,
are apparently disapproving of and putting up with. Which
would be understandable if we were still in the 1950s and
men didn't want equal rights, but they DO now! Not all of
them, maybe, but most of them – our brothers, fathers and
sons – THEY believe this. To be a feminist should never
be an insult, or anything close to one, and yet here we are.
We're at the point where it feels like we've created a delicious
chocolate bar and wrapped it up and packaged it under the
title 'human shit'. A great product, that no one wants.

Look around you. Stop and ask the person next to you,
wherever you are right now, whether he, she or it believes
in equality of the sexes – they will say yes. They just will.
But then you need to ask them if they would identify as a
feminist. There's a fairly big chance they will say no because,
for whatever reason, they don't reckon they are. Maybe they
feel they're not passionate enough, or they're not prepared to
physically fight. Maybe they feel they won't be accepted, or
they're scared of being seen as a 'man hater' or being called
'butch' and 'aggressive' behind their backs, or maybe they
don't like that it's got the word 'feminine' in it – whatever
it is, it's irrelevant. The fact is this: people are disassociating
themselves with the word and that's wrong. For the sake of
making a positive change, I'm up for a new word if you are.
What do you think about *equalists?* I think it has a certain
ring to it, don't you?

So, *equalists* . . . what do you say? Room for one more?
One more to help us fight the good fight? One more
who's ready to stand up and take this head on – not just
big business and government, but ready to fight for the
girl who isn't ready to fight for herself yet? The girl who's
embarrassed, or depressed, or left out. Who's ready to fight
with me for the normal girl?

Of course there's room; in a fight this important there's
room for everyone. So let's get going, shall we?

Em xx

Dear Trump

I didn't vote for you. Even if I could have I would have chosen to choke on my hair for the rest of my life rather than vote for you. Your presence in the White House has made me ashamed of the world. But in a weird sort of way I'm happy you're there. Because the fact that YOU, Mr Trump, a bigoted, racist, sexist, power-hungry, homophobe were elected has evoked a backlash from the people that has proven more powerful than we could have ever thought possible. Although in lots of ways I'm ashamed of the American public; their response, the world's response to the decision to make you president, has been unbelievable, it has been powerful, it has been uniting and it has reminded me, at a time when I needed reminding, that love will always win. You may be president, you may be there by public demand, but you are hated by so many. So many people who, had it not have been for you, would not have united as they have and stood together to fight for what is right.

I have a feeling that you and your term as president will be the cloud from which the brightest rainbow will emerge. A rainbow that will adorn flags that will fly from every window; a rainbow that will show the world that kindness has won.

And so, in the words of a Deep South-residing white

American man, who risked his life to save his black best friend, Forrest Gump: that's all I've got to say about that.

Regards,

Em

Dear Topshop

cc All high street shops
FAO: Sir Philip, PR team, designers, marketing, shop assistants

Please forgive my writing like this but there are a couple of things I really need to get off my chest. I'm writing to you on behalf of women everywhere – women who like your clothes and enjoy your brand but have been known, on occasion, to leave your store crying. Women who have been forced to shop elsewhere because your clothes don't fit and women who probably ought to apologise for damaging various items of clothing by getting stuck in them. I would very much like to voice the concerns of us women in the hope that you'll take a good hard look at yourselves. I also hope that you will share this letter among your high-street friends, because this is very much their problem too.

I wanted to start by talking to you about last summer. Last summer two terrible things happened to me on Oxford Street. The first, something I still have slightly hysterical nightmares about, involved me getting stuck in a Miss Selfridge size 12 crop-top; the second resulted in a 'fuck off, Topshop (sorry), I fucking hate you (sorry) and Philip Green, you can go and die (sorry)' type explosion at your security guard because all your clothes were labelled wrong. (I'm not

very good at confrontation. Philip Green, I don't actually
want you to die.)

I don't know why I was on Oxford Street in the first
place; I'm not a religious person but I can only imagine that
if I did find myself on the Road To Hell, this would be my
destination. What I do know, however, is that I was going
to Glastonbury the next day and didn't have nearly enough
Aztec-patterned clothing to pull off 'festival chic'. So there
I was, in Miss Selfridge, with my mum, bejewelled garment
stuck somewhere between tit and throat, sweating like a pig
for twenty minutes as we wrestled it off me.

I don't know if this is a situation you have personally
found yourself in, but just in case you haven't, let me set
the scene for you: it was hot and I was in a changing room.
I was feeling frizzy and fat and would rather have plucked
out all my arm hairs one by one than dragged my sweaty
ass round London, but there I was. I pulled said shirt over
my head and realised fairly quickly that my head was the
only thing this item was getting over in a hurry. I pulled
and I pulled but to no avail. It was then I caught sight of
myself in the mirror . . .

You know when you get out of a REALLY hot shower
and see yourself in the mirror and you're all blotchy?
Imagine that happening after you've taken a whole load of
magic mushrooms. That was me. With one tit squeezed
into the fabric and the other squished out the bottom, I
had the boob equivalent of a very lazy eye. As I caught
the eye of the marshmallow staring back at me, all I could
think was: you poor mess, no one will ever, EVER, find

you attractive. And at that moment I was right. I was, for
a small moment, the most unattractive person in all the
land, because I couldn't find one thing I was looking at and
didn't loathe.

And that's just it, isn't it? If you look at yourself in the
mirror and genuinely can't stand the person staring back at
you; if every time you look at yourself you die a bit inside,
then no, no one *will* ever find you attractive, because you
won't let them.

In life, however, we've all found little ways of stifling our
self-loathing. It's still there, it still eats away at us, but as long
as we can shy away from mirrors, un-tag photos or wear
baggy jumpers, we are able to sweep it under the rug.

In fact, we are able to let this little mound under the rug
do its thing, for days, weeks, sometimes months, walking
around it, pretending it's not there. We're able to ignore it
even as it becomes so enormous that eventually the entire
room the rug covers become unusable, but that's OK,
because it's at that point that we shut the door.

And then we come and visit you. We go shopping. We
take off our clothes; we stand in front of the mirror and
have absolutely nowhere to hide. No corners, no rugs, no
flattering lighting and no 'block' button. We are confronted
with our bodies and all their wibbly-wobbly bits and the
door smashes open and we run full speed at the rug, which
explodes, and every little bit of self-doubt and self-hate
comes pouring out, drenching us in the most depressing
metaphorical wave ever.

And that's shopping in a nutshell. It's not always quite as

dramatic as this, but it is exposing and honest in a way we don't like because we, as girls, aren't very good at 'dealing' with things. 'Hate My Body' is something we can generally put on tomorrow's to-do list, silently celebrating the fact that tomorrow never comes, but sometimes we can't help it. And in that moment, with a very lovely, if not very condescending woman (who I can only hope actually worked at Miss Selfridge) on one side, and Mum on the other, I have never hated my body more.

I didn't buy the top in the end, although I probably ought to have paid for it, considering the damage I did getting it off. (If you see Miss Selfridge around, please do apologise.) It was nice though, and had they had it in a bigger size (12 was all they had in store), I definitely would have bought it. But, as we are beginning to see more and more in your high-street shops these days, they didn't. As Katie Hopkins put it: 'a size 12 is a size called fat' – and Miss Selfridge'll be damned if it attracts the fatties.

So this brings me to my second terrible Oxford Street experience of the summer: you.

My sister is really tall. She is five years my junior and five inches taller, (I think I must have been a product of the milkman) and she's got the sort of legs that finish just underneath her enormous boobs. Yep, I know, I know, lucky girl, except not really . . . because she actually has one of the hardest bodies to dress in that she does not meet 'conventional' sizing standards. All we came in for was a pair of high-waisted denim shorts, which, considering we were looking for the product of the summer in the biggest branch of Topshop in the country, you might have thought would have been easy enough.

You would have been wrong. Despite being a size 14, Katya couldn't fit into any of the shorts in your shop, and when we asked the ridiculously surly shop assistant if you stocked anything bigger, we were met with the sort of reaction you would expect from someone who had just found out they'd been eating nothing but human shit disguised as food for the last three years. You didn't have anything bigger.

It was really fucking depressing. So, as we left, I made her turn around to your bolshie-ass security guard and the swarms of confused tourists and stressed-out shoppers and literally tell Topshop to fuck off. Tell it to die, tell Philip Green he's a twat. Tell them that you didn't want their shorts anyway. Tell them that you're going to shit through their letterbox. Tell them that you're better than them.

With hindsight, it's a wonder we didn't get arrested. (Thank you for not arresting us.)

But for a small minute there it made us feel better – we were taking back a little bit of control, letting you soul-destroying size-ist bastards know that we didn't need you, that we were the masters of our own happiness and that you weren't going to make us feel shit anymore. Bam. How's that for girl power? Germaine Greer, eat your heart out.

But then, of course, as we walked (were ushered) away from Topshop and back through the crowds of Oxford Street, the sun came out and Kat didn't have any shorts and I didn't have any Aztec. And it was just depressing again.

And so, riddle me this: are you OK with that? Are you OK with the fact that when I asked my sixteen-year-old sister if she wanted to do anything about it, she replied with this: 'What am I going to do about it? So what, I write a letter to Philip Green and he reads it and thinks, Oh, poor fat chick, and then nothing happens?'

Because you shouldn't be. This is NOT OK.

Oh, and I'm just getting started. Of the 100 women I asked, seventy of them said they too had cried in a shop changing room at some point in their lives. This is happening on your watch, guys. Whether we're interested in fashion or not, I'm sure you're aware that we all NEED clothes, and it is of course your job to ensure that we all NEED YOUR clothes, which you're doing a sterling job of making sure that we do, but more on that later.

Every single sexist cliché under the sun tells us that shopping is our one true calling in life yet, here we are, dreading the day we bend over too far and hear that all-too-familiar ripping sound that can mean only one thing: jeans shopping. The one type of shopping guaranteed to make me cry. Can you imagine if Waitrose made us cry? Or Ikea? What gives you the right to accept this as a 'thing'?

Actually, more to the point, can you imagine this happening in Topman? (Please forward this particular section to all the women in the office.)

'Are you alright, Dave? You've been in there for ages . . .'

'Yep, all good, just gimme a sec!'

'Are you sure, mate? It's alright if you're not, you know, this shop always makes me feel rubbish and the lighting in these rooms can be so unforgiving.'

'Carl, shuttup, I told you, I'm fine.'

'I know, bud. I'm just saying ... shall I go and wait outside?'

'Yeah. Wait, no! Don't go ... oh mate, I hate this! I feel horrible and nothing fits right and everything makes me feel fat and ugly and no one's ever going to love me if I can't even get my stupid arse into a pair of jeans.'

'Oh Dave, bro, don't talk like that ... it's fine, it's all fine, here look, let me help ... oh hey! Look at you, you look great!'

'No I don't, I look fat. I want to go home now ... can you help me undo this?'

NEVER NEVER NEVER. Here is what really happens:

'Hey mate, are you going to try that on?'

'Nah bro, it's in my size. Imma just get it now.'

'Cool.'

'Cool.'

Done.

Is it a completely inconceivable notion that this could happen on both sides of your store?

Now, I don't know how your office works but my research showed that, generally speaking, women occupy a third of jobs in the fashion industry. This doesn't seem like an awful lot; it would appear that women are discriminated against in your line of work, which is ironic, if you ask me, since this is our 'thang' and all, but that's not why I brought it up. I brought it up because a third is actually quite a lot. Enough to make a difference at least, however small that difference may be.

But I'm still waiting on that difference. I'm still waiting for the big reveal where you all go 'PUNKED – ahaha, you thought we didn't care and that we wanted you to be unhappy and feel depressed every time you come into our shops . . . we're only messing, here, look, come this way, check it out, a rack with clothes from size 6 to size 26, the way it should be. Oh girls, we really got you there. I bet you thought we'd all gone totally mad!'

But since this hasn't happened yet, and I've been waiting a while, I can only assume that you HAVE gone totally mad. The person who decided that size 16 shorts didn't belong on the rails in your stores may not have been a woman, but it will have been okayed by one. Or one hundred. Apparently someone has conveniently forgotten about the time that THEY cried in a changing room?

When I was younger I did most of my shopping with my mum. Obviously I couldn't afford anything that I was shopping for and everything from school uniform to jeans shopping was something we did together. I have a longstanding joke with my boyfriend that Ikea is where relationships go to die. If you can come out of there still as in love as when you went in, then you should get married and have lots of babies immediately. In fact, where the café

currently is at the checkout they ought to have an altar and
a priest for those people who come out smiling. Because
you haven't seen a couple fight until you've seen them with
a measuring tape and a colour chart. I think shopping with
your mum is the same. You take out anger you didn't even
know you had on your nearest and dearest, and for me at
least that is my mum.

She stood patiently waiting outside every fitting room
cubicle with the same jeans in varying sizes for the first
sixteen years of my life, and I gave her absolute hell. I would
cry and scream and shout at her. I would ungraciously grab
my stomach rolls and shove them in her face telling her I
hated myself and everything in my life.

And she would stand there and say all the right things; she
would hold my hand and cuddle me and stay with me for as
long as it took. Sometimes she would tell me to shut up, but
she mostly kept her cool and did her very best to make me as
happy as possible.

But it's only now, in the last couple of years, as I have
shopped with my sister and looked back at my own
experiences, that I realise how utterly horrendous that
must have been for her to witness. She's always told me
that, as a mother, you are only ever as happy as your
unhappiest child and, although I'm a fair few years off
becoming a mother myself, it's something I'm beginning
to understand.

When I scream at her and tell her that I hate myself, there
is literally nothing she can do. As I sob she is completely
powerless, unable to make me feel any better, and we both

leave as unhappy as each other. Except, when I get home,
I can wipe the whole experience from memory, sweeping
it unceremoniously under that rug – but for Mum, she gets
home and relives it over and over again, worrying about it,
worrying that I'm unhappy.

All because I couldn't get into a pair of jeans.

And so I want to know this: are you women who are
making these decisions also forgetting about the times you
took your daughters, friends and sisters to the changing
rooms?

You no doubt use the rug to hide your shit from
yourself when you get home, but what do you do with
other people's pain? Still now I get the most horrible
twisting in my stomach when I remember my sister crying
to me because she couldn't find any clothes that fit her.
We were on holiday and had to go to a cocktail party . . .
she won't even remember it but Jesus Christ it broke my
heart.

So even if by some really weird coincidence the fashion
industry is made up exclusively of the 30 per cent of
women that haven't cried in a changing room, basic
mathematics suggests you will have been with someone
who has.

And so you must be mad. Or evil. Because if I had any say
in the happiness of my future daughters or any of her friends,
I would do something, anything I could. And yes, I do
realise I sound like the biggest drama queen in the country,
but it is almost as serious as I'm making it out to be. Because
since no one is making a difference, and no changes are

being made, and no one is taking a stand, I have to assume
that you're all insane.

But do you want to know what makes me certain that
you're crazy? Like, what *really* makes me sure? 'Plus size'. The
fact that 'plus size' is even a thing makes me know you are
all insane. I want to find the inventor of 'plus size' and have
them sectioned. Plus Size. PLUS SIZE. What do you mean,
plus size?

'You are BIGGER than a size. Like, there isn't a
measurement for you yet. We know the size of a car, and a
house, and a park, and the sea; we even know the size of the
moon, but you, *eesh*, there is no size for you . . . we're just
going to call you 'plus' size – like size, only a bit bigger. Is
that OK? Good.'

GOOD? NO! NOT GOOD. NOT GOOD AT ALL.

The national average for women in the UK is a size 16,
which some companies consider 'plus size'. So I can only
assume at least some (theoretically half) of the women
working in your shop can't actually shop there because
nothing will fit.

I remember when I was little Mum used to dress me head-
to-toe in Little Boden – honestly, it was adorable and I lived
for the day my floral T-shirts would arrive in the post. But
then I got older and I started to shop where Mum shopped:
Fat Face and White Stuff. (She wasn't very cool back then
and, as a result, nor was I.) I must have been the only
thirteen-year-old in the world to have three different colours
of Birkenstocks. (Pale blue, white and pink, just in case you
were interested.)

It's the classic teenage woe: I HATE ALL MY CLOTHES! But for me it was a real problem. We recently took them all to a charity shop and I think even they were sceptical. I'm not actually sure where all my friends were doing their shopping at the time but I remember the day I went to my big school to take my design and technology scholarship (told you I wasn't very cool), Mum introduced me to you, Topshop, and it was then that I bought my first ever 'fashionable' piece of clothing.

I was twelve and EXCITED. It was a white, heavy cotton top, with dark blue and black flowers on it. It had long, random pieces of material that started at the waistband just underneath my boobs and floated oh so ridiculously to the hem. I think I only got rid of it last year. I wore it everywhere. Literally, it was the coolest thing I had ever owned and the label made it very special.

It felt really good to be in on the secret. To have a top that the older girls had – maybe even one that had appeared in a magazine. (Please remember up until then the clothes I was wearing at the time were only ever seen on people who went on walking holidays.)

So over time I began to replace and upgrade everything in my wardrobe so that now, ten years later, I'm happy with (nearly) everything in there. I also enjoy knowing that most of my friends will have the same Topshop Leigh jeans (you did well with those) as me, and that we've all got at least one of the same shirts. I like shopping with my friends. I like it when someone asks me where my dress is from and I can proudly tell them. I like it when they ask to borrow something they've seen and liked.

Clothes are really important, they make us feel good and help us break a lot of ice with people we don't know that well or like that much. They give us something to talk about and something to do. They're an enormous part of our lives. So when I was little and felt uncool in my Fat Face T-shirts, White Stuff khaki skirts and whatever Birkenstocks took my fancy that day, I felt left out and I felt different.

So how do you suppose it feels to know that you CAN'T shop in the 'cool' shops, even if your mum did take you there? How do you think it feels to be fifteen years old, already feeling different and self-conscious because you're bigger than everybody else and all your friends are going to the high-street shops and you can't go? I reckon it feels really rubbish, and by making 'plus size' a thing, and by not stocking certain sizes in your shops, that is what you are doing.

So, since you aren't doing the job well enough, plus size shops such as Simply B and Evans have stepped up and, although I'm sure there are some hidden gems in the racks, I'm not sure they classify as 'cool'. In fact, I know they're not cool. And at a time of your life when being 'cool' is paramount, to be left with 'uncool' or nothing has got to be horrendous.

But what's terrifying is that we don't actually have a choice in this. It's not like a size 18 could start wearing only your clothes in an act of defiance; she literally couldn't. She is being prevented from doing something solely on the grounds of her appearance. By you.

Is this your plan for girly shopping trips five years from now:

'Oh, I really need a dress for my party tomorrow night.'
  'Me too!'
  'So do I!'
  'Cool, so shall we reconvene here in like twenty minutes?'
  'Yup, I'm off to Fat And Depressed, where are you going, Kriss?'
  'So Thin It's Dangerous . . . what about you, Louise?'
  'Er, think I'm going to hit up Thunder Thighs R Us. Catch up with you guys later!'

A lot of people have spoken out about how girls of a certain size ought to be made to feel 'uncomfortable' when they can't find a size that'll fit. But what I don't think people understand is that they are already uncomfortable. We are all uncomfortable most the time. The argument is that by stocking bigger clothes, shops are 'facilitating an unhealthy lifestyle', but that makes no sense. Because they're not. They are literally facilitating people getting dressed and perhaps not crying as they do it. By the very nature of the demand for 'plus size' (we have GOT to rename that) shops, the 'problem' is already here and a size 18 is not going to wake up tomorrow a size 8 because Karen Millen didn't have anything for her. She'll just wake up feeling really unhappy.

As one wise teenage girl told me: 'We accommodate

people who are born skinny, so why would you then not accommodate people who were born curvy?' Good question. So WHAT are you going to do about it?

And it's not just a plus size problem, you know. It's all labels. Everyone is so obsessed with labels – your labels. I remember a few years ago I was working for the military charity Tickets for Troops, and was invited to go to the James Bond *Skyfall* première – a pretty badass event by anyone's standards and I needed to look good . . . you know how it is.

Anyway, it was winter, it was cold, and so I ran into the closest Topshop branch to my office. (Will I ever learn?) It was the ultimate winter shopping experience – you know, when it's really cold outside and you're wearing all the clothes in your wardrobe and then you go into a shop that is reaching Sahara temperatures? And then you start to sweat. And stress. Why do you make it so hot in there, by the way? Please get back to me on this one.

So I picked up a dress and ran into the changing room. The lovely (no, she really was!) shop assistant helped me into this dress and, as she looked at me in the mirror, I kid you not, she said, 'I think you need a size smaller.' *Ahahah*, sorry, what? 'Yes please thank you very much and I love you, I'll take it.' Didn't even try the fucker on. Just bought it 'cos I NEEDED A SIZE SMALLER. I was very much a size 12 (probably a 14 if we're being honest) at the time and BAM! I could fit into a 10. Sixty-five pounds I paid. For a compliment. I spent £65 on a fucking compliment. What is wrong with me?

As it turned out, the dress looked *crackalacking* . . . a bit 'titty' for a work do, but it's done me about 100 parties since then, so I really can't complain. But that is so beside the point. I am the shallowest person in the whole world and I literally bought a dress because the shop assistant implied I was thin. That I could fit into a thin person dress. What a weird thought process.

And you know what? I really wish this had only happened once. But it keeps happening! For my eighteenth birthday my mum bought me a really gorgeous skirt in a size 10 (YOURS AGAIN!) and it didn't fit. Not even CLOSE. Literally didn't even get halfway up my thighs, but did I take it back? Did I fuck. I turned twenty-one and it still hangs in my wardrobe waiting for the day I lose enough weight to fit into it.

I think I managed to get it on once, first thing in the morning after I'd spent three days in bed with a bug. I moved house not that long ago and ebayed a whole load of my stuff, but for some reason I couldn't let this skirt go; it hangs in my wardrobe every day, judging me. Laughing at me. (I can actually do it up now, by the way, but it still gives a muffin top Delia would be proud of.)

And this isn't just me. Countless women I've spoken to have told me that they bought things that didn't fit properly just because of the label; that they've kept things that don't fit in the hope they'll shrink into them. As one sixteen-year-old girl told me, 'I always look for a small size first. I don't know why but if I buy something in a size 8 I feel better about myself.'

And that, my judgey friends, is not OK. Why does she feel better about herself in a size 8 than in a size 12? Actually, more to the point, why is it that she can fit into both? You've got a serious problem with your sizing and you need to understand how depressing it is that online you'll say 'model wears size 8' and then a size 8 person orders it and looks like mashed potato.

One of our Pretty Normal Me readers told me that if she had one complaint about Topshop it would, 'One hundred per cent be how ridiculously skinny the legs on the models are. This means every time I go in there I'll think how nice a pair of trousers are but when I put them on they always make me feel huge, even if I buy a size up.'

And that's another lady leaving your shop feeling sad. And so, Philip, designers, PR team, interns, shop assistants, I am IMPLORING you to make a change here. It is simply not good enough that you're making people feel rubbish and getting away with it.

It is beyond me why we are so accepting of this, but it might be worth remembering that if you do intend to keep flourishing as a business you should know that half the British female population is unable to wear your clothes. The obesity epidemic may well be a problem, but it certainly isn't yours. What IS your problem however are the hordes of young girls being made to feel left out and different directly as a result of your decisions.

So I'm offering you an ultimatum – you can either walk around every single school in the country and individually tell every girl of size 16 and up, face to face, that they are not welcome in your stores because they are too fat, or you can start accepting this for what it is and do your very best to make this right.

And while you're at it, I would strongly recommend designing clothes for the people who are going to wear them. It's no good putting a size 14 item on the rack that you made for a size 6. So that's got to stop. (And you need to find a space in shirts for tits to go.)

I don't know if you really understand the magnitude of this problem. I hope I've highlighted some key issues in this letter, but the power really is in your hands here. This is your time to make a change. Be the good guy. Hell, get a size 12 model in, and not just to show off the maternity range.

I dabbled with the idea of orchestrating a boycott, but you're too strong; you're like heroin for teenagers. It would never work and I know you know that, which is why you don't feel like you need to do anything.

So these are my terms:

- Stock bigger sizes (you'll need to talk this one through with the others).
- Have one item of every size on your rails. I don't care if it's expensive; this is a sacrifice you need to make.
- Hire more sensitive shop assistants. Or just teach the ones you've got to be nicer.
- Get some cellulite in your campaigns – how you haven't been done for false advertising yet I don't know.
- THINK OF THE CHILDREN.

I don't know what I'll do if you don't agree to them – and let's face it, you probably won't – but please, please, *pleeeeeease*, Sir Philip, I am BEGGING you to do the right thing here.

And fast.

Em

Dear Cat-callers

Shut the fuck up.
Yours sincerely,

Womankind

Dear Hollywood

cc All casting directors, producers, make-up artists, costume designers and directors

So, I've got some questions for you – questions I hope cause you to have a long hard think about the state of affairs in your weird, often wonderful and totally ridiculous world. Here goes:

- Why is it that women in films always wake up with lip-gloss on?
- Why is it that after sex women are somehow able to just pull down their skirts/up their jeans and crack on with their days as normal without having to deal with any **hrhumm** mess?
- Along the same lines, why does no film show the mandatory I-don't-want-to-get-cystitis-wee after they've finished their unrealistically passionate shag?
- Why is it that even if our female lead is sweating from her eyeballs, she still somehow has better hair than I could ever hope for?
- On the same theme, why is it that these women also somehow manage to wake up with the most perfect hair EVER?! And that even if it is 'bed-head' it's still

so goddamn sexy and doesn't explode into a ball of frizz when she runs a brush through it?

- Again with the hair, because I can't let it go, why is it that even if a girl is shown to have like *totally* let herself go and is seen out and about in 'sweatpants', she will still be guaranteed to have the glossiest, flowiest hair in all of the land?
- Why is it that the only time I saw a spot on a girl was in *Angus, Thongs and Perfect Snogging* all those years ago? Does no one get spots anymore? And if not, why not? Please share with me their secrets.
- Also, why is it that these girls can all eat so much mac'n'cheese and pizza like every night and yet still have the best body/hair/skin combinations I've ever seen?
- Why is it that there is usually one really unfit girl who has *never ever* been on a run before who, despite this, has the best calves in the country? Fine, great that you want an 'unfit' character, but please make her look the part. (Casting would be easier . . .)
- Where do her toned abs come from?
- And also, why is it that when this aforementioned girl hits a pivotal moment in her life/plotline and the music swells, that she is able to contemplate all of her decisions while on a really long run that doesn't cause her to break a sweat, ruin her hair, or choke up a lung?
- How are these women able to do EVERYTHING in high heels without so much as mentioning the fact that she hasn't felt her feet in four days?

- Why does no one ever fall asleep with a contact lens in?
- How come every makeover in every film is complete after removing the character's glasses and straightening her hair? (I draw your attention to the *Princess Diaries* – WE ALL KNOW THAT ANNE HATHAWAY IS A NATURAL STUNNER!)
- Why are they all wearing matching underwear? WHO has time? Most of us can't manage matching flipping socks.
- Why is it that when our girl gets out of the shower she never has any remnants of last night's make-up on her cheeks?
- How does her bar job generate enough cash to not only pay for an amazing apartment but one that is full of stuff? I've lived in my flat for ages and the walls are still basically empty because photo frames are a luxury whereas food is my necessity.
- Ooh, this is a big one. WHY ARE HANGOVERS SO BADLY MISREPRESENTED? When I'm hungover I need a full-fat coke, a packet of ready-salted Hula Hoops and a sofa ASAP. Somehow though, in your world, hungover women have a sixty-second ritual:

   10 seconds to hold their temples.
   10 seconds to look for their phones and realise they are late for something.
   10 seconds to work out where they are.

10 seconds to push aside all the beer cans/the man next to them.

10 seconds to have a flashback.

10 seconds to get out of bed.

Hey presto. Sixty-second hangover complete.

- Why does everyone bump into each other everywhere?
- Why is every bar full of hot single men who somehow aren't at all creepy even though they've been staring at our main girl for a whole scene and are neither asked to confirm or deny if they have slipped something into the drink they just bought for her. NO QUESTIONS ASKED.
- Why does no woman ever seem to need to do body hair maintenance, like ever? *Bridget Jones* was the ONLY time I saw a woman acknowledge that, after a long time as a singleton, she needed to take care of the fur.
- No pony-tail kink? How? If my hair has been tied up and I let it down I look like I've been crimped. One slow-motion flick and they're all salon fresh? I don't buy it.
- Oh, and also, you know those times where the girl stays at a guy's house for like a week, skipping out on all of her commitments in favour of lots of sex and nice moments in his crisp white shirts? Where and how does she poo?

These questions are endless because I cannot stop thinking of all of the times your bullshit reading was off the chart.

And I don't mean or particularly care about the 'well, how did he get there so quickly? It's Friday night leaving London, he would DEFINITELY have got stuck in traffic; wait, hang on, have you guys noticed that he hasn't had a wee yet, like ALL film? Pfft. No way, as if he would keep that gun in his belt with the safety off . . . urgh, that wouldn't happen; cars don't even explode these days. Wait, how does he even have her number? They've only met once' questions that we find ourselves asking every time we sit down to watch James Bond.

I mean your bog-standard representation of what are supposed to be real, NORMAL women. Because if what you're showing to be normal is legit what we are supposed to be doing, then there is so much fundamentally wrong with everything that I do.

Now before you panic, don't worry, I understand that I'm basically pissing in the wind here and that you would probably lose quite a lot of money if you did dedicate half the film to showing the days when people didn't really do anything. The days when they forget to buy dishwasher salt, when they accidently eat gluten and have to spend a few days nursing the beach ball that is their stomach, when, try as they might, they cannot make their hair play ball and it looks a bit meh until they next wash it. So I won't ask for half the film. But I'd like to put the case forward for a quarter of it.

Just the occasional shot of a character checking out the

'still fresh' aisle of her local supermarket, of her hugging her boyfriend and leaving a huge smudge of make-up on his shirt and maybe even, if you can face it, just a glimpse of the slightly less sexy, less glamorous side to sex?

Because, by not doing any of this, we are setting a LOT of girls up for some catastrophic disappointments when they reach adulthood and realise that working in a pub won't enable them to move out of home; that not every man in every big city they go to will fall in love with them, and that sometimes life, like our faces and our bodies, isn't perfect.

They're not stupid. They're not expecting a happily ever after; they're not expecting to kiss a frog and get a prince; they're not expecting to be rescued. So your plotlines are safe. But a few home truths? A bit of reality? Would that really be the end of the world? C'monnnn, *pleeeeease*?

I'll tell you what, as a baby-step how does this sound: why not cast a 'curvy' girl as the lead in a romcom? And not in an ironic way, or in a film that is all about her being 'fat' and how she needs to overcome that – and don't make it Rebel Wilson or Melissa McCarthy, who you have already typecast as big women who can only play characters as such – but just a woman who kind of looks a bit chubby who isn't defined by that. Does that sound easy enough? (Trick question. You are the legends that can CGI the whole of California falling down . . . this is definitely easy enough.)

I hope you've heard what I've said, because we could really use a break.

If you're looking for any more in the way of inspiration, or even a director to ensure this is all done properly, you know where I am.

* *Insert epic, profound and cheesy final line here*** ***

Em

Dear Every Single One Of My Jumpers

Thank you. For hiding last night's three puddings from me and from the world, thank you.

Em

Dear Janis Joplin

cc *Little Mix, Miley Cyrus, Ariana Grande etc. etc. etc.*

'You can destroy your now by worrying about tomorrow.'
I've always loved this quote and I've always loved you for
saying it. Why stress about something that you can't fix?
Why waste your time worrying about something out of your
control? If you might die tomorrow, then why not live life
to the fullest today? That, to me, epitomises everything you
were, everything you represented. That to me, epitomises
rock'n'roll.

As I write this letter I'm sitting cross-legged on the floor,
my hair is impossibly wild after an hour in the rain and I'm
listening to your *Greatest Hits* album. Your music is doing
a number of things to me: it is relaxing and inspiring me
in equal measure, it is making me wish I was sitting on a
doorstep in Haight Ashbury in the sunshine and not in a
cul-de-sac in Windsor, and it's making me *really* wish I was
writing this love letter to you dressed in something oversized
and floaty, chain-smoking unfiltered cigarettes and drinking
Southern Comfort from the bottle. It makes me long for
your carefree nature, your passion for life, your raw talent.

I close my eyes and I can no longer hear my boyfriend's
mum telling him how she has started crocheting again. I stop

worrying about missing rush hour as I plan my route back to London this evening, and I really don't care that I have no make-up on and that I have spots all over my chin. I don't mind that my bank balance is pitifully small, that I have deadlines weighing down on me from everywhere; I don't care that tomorrow is Monday. I don't worry about what I'm going to wear to my meeting in the morning, that I've lost my phone charger or the fact that I'm a few weeks overdue getting my bikini-line done. I listen to your music and it drowns out the mundane monotony and stress of my reality.

Despite having loved you since I first heard 'Mercedes Benz' aged about ten, I know very little about you. I know that you were from Texas, I know that you were a heroin addict and I know you died, like so many other musical greats, far, far too young at the age of twenty-seven. I don't know who you were dating, I don't know where you liked to do your shopping or if your parents resented your success. I don't know what nightclubs you frequented, how often you got your hair cut or what filter you would have used on Instagram. I don't know what the inside of your house looked like, how much money you had or what size your breasts were. I never knew anything about you – you died before my time and, actually, you died before any of this would have been any of my business. And as a result, all I know about you is what your music tells me. When it comes to you I am left with nothing but your lyrics, your passion and some grainy black-and-white photos with which to paint my mental picture. And what a beautiful picture it is.

I was born in 1994, twenty-four years after you had died,

and I spend a lot of time wishing I had been born earlier.
The song that was number one on the day I was born was
called 'Love Is All Around' by a band called Wet Wet Wet,
and it only went downhill from there. Throughout my
childhood my heroes all had bad highlights, no clothes on
and sung songs that were written for them by other people.
The first song I remember dancing to at a school disco was
called 'The Ketchup Song', I shit you not. One of my first
heroes, Britney Spears, was made famous by a song called
'Hit Me Baby One More Time'; my favourite music video of
the time was a song called 'Dirrty' (two Rs, not sure why)
in which the singer, Christina Aguilera, was wearing ass-less
chaps and, unless you knew how to shake your prepubescent
bum to a song called 'Bootylicious' performed by a band
called Destiny's Child, then you just weren't worth knowing.
The first gig I went to with my friends was to see a group
called Girls Aloud and their most famous song at the time
was called 'Something Kinda Oooh' – says it all really,
doesn't it? And believe it or not, it's got even worse since
then. At some point, probably in the 1990s, female musicians
were told that if they wanted to sell records or 'make it' in
an incredibly competitive industry then they were going
to need to do it basically naked. The younger you are, the
skinnier and the sluttier, the better.

Of course women have always been sexualised in the
music industry – a couple of photos into my Google search
of you just now has shown me your breasts – but what we've
got going on at the moment is madness. At some point it
stopped being about the music, it pretty much stopped being

about talent and it definitely stopped being about art. There's still some beautiful music being created, don't get me wrong, you did inspire something totally amazing, but the industry as a whole? You wouldn't recognise it.

Despite the fact that we're surrounded by less than suitable role models at the moment, we are still being encouraged to look up to them. Young girls are able to twerk (a dance move pioneered by a teen pop star called Miley Cyrus, which basically requires you to shake your arse in every conceivable direction) only months after they've learned how to walk; they can recite the words to songs they thankfully don't understand the meaning of in the playground, and if you ask any of these young girls what they want to be when they grow up they all say the same thing: 'When I grow up, I want to be famous.' A band called the Pussycat Dolls (don't even get me started) sung about it a few years ago; that was the title, all about being 'a star' and a 'number one chick'.

I'd like to think they were being ironic, but the more I think about it, I'm not so sure. The world of music has changed so dramatically. God, it makes me miss you.

The closest we came to an artist like you in recent years was a woman called Amy Winehouse. She was a true legend, a beautiful artist and troubled soul who, like you and so many before her, succumbed to a life of drink and drugs, which saw her join the infamous '27 Club'. She died on 23 July 2011 and it broke my heart. I felt a huge loss, I wore only black for three days and I felt the way millions must have felt when they lost you. The way the world feels when it loses a true artist who spoke to us on an emotional level.

Amy Winehouse spoke to me, she really spoke to me, and she was the only artist to have done that in my lifetime. Bearing in my mind what I told you about 'The Ketchup Song', I suppose that's not entirely surprising.

The world has told me that I shouldn't look up to you; everything I have been taught in my little life says that you shouldn't be a role model – you were a smoker, a drinker, a heroin addict. Your addictions killed you. And yet, I'm looking around me, I'm looking for women to look up to, I'm looking for an artist, I'm looking for passion and for love and I've found myself lost in a sea of high-waisted knickers, hair extensions and auto-tune. Somehow, the only women I've found to aspire to in this industry have been those so ready to sacrifice themselves for their art that they've been killed by it. Somehow, the clean-cut, butter wouldn't melt, I've never got shitfaced in my life (but for a price I'll film myself having sex and leak it to the *Sunday Mirror*) role models of today just haven't cut it, and instead I find myself admiring and wishing for the days of sex, drugs and rock'n'roll. Honest, dirty, beautiful. I look up to you, I look up to Amy, and I admire you in ways I didn't think I could admire a person.

Perhaps I sound mad; perhaps it is safer for young girls to be looking up to women whose biggest crime is a juicing cleanse and a skirt four inches too short, and that by admitting I miss women so lost in addiction that it killed them I'll be forbidden from having children or selling this book to anyone under the age of eighteen but, here I am, missing you, longing for you, looking up to you.

You said once about your singing: 'When I sing, I feel like when you're first in love. It's more than sex. It's that point two people can get to they call love, when you really touch someone for the first time, but it's gigantic, multiplied by the whole audience. I feel chills.'

By comparison, artist Miley Cyrus (the aforementioned creator of the 'twerk') was once quoted saying this about her art: 'When preparing for a concert, I do lots of training. I work with a choreographer to create great moves and then I have to keep my voice strong with lessons.'

And that's not art, that's not what music is about, that isn't the world you left all those years ago.

To die for your art is beauty, to die for your art is passion, to die for your art is sacrifice and, Janis, I want to thank you for your sacrifice.

All my love and adoration,

Em xxxx

Dear Online Trolls

FAO: anyone still living in their mother's basement

Right you lot, first things first: out of your mothers'
basements now please. I know you feel like a big man or a
hard bitch down there but imma need for you all to prise
your RSI-riddled fingers off that sticky keyboard of yours,
stand up, see if you have any feeling left in your arse, and
make your way past the countless empty cartons of smelly,
off Chinese takeaways and read this letter in the real world –
outside maybe, or at least on my level (above ground).
Because you, you little shits, have to my mind wreaked *quite*
enough havoc as of late and I am saying 'enough'.

I'm Em, by the way, although to your kind I'm more
commonly known as something slightly different: mostly
fat, often talentless, definitely spoilt and occasionally a bitch?
Ringing any bells, or have you been SO busy tearing women
down that we're all just blurring into one big target? You
have been ripping into me, quite unfairly (in my humble
opinion) for the last six years. You've been doing it since I was
seventeen and still at school and hadn't done anything more
noteworthy with my life than make it into a background shot
of *Top of the Pops* when Daniel Powter was performing 'Bad
Day' back in the early 2000s, and it wasn't like any of you

recognised me from my offbeat arm waving. Nope, you were having a go at me quite simply because I had a famous dad, and you reckoned that because of this I was fair game.

I'm pretty sure I can handle any abuse you send my way these days because at least I feel I might be doing something to merit it – as in I have an opinion, a social media presence of sorts and a blog. But I have a hard time believing that I deserve any of it, not least because it started when I was just a child. So I thought, just to refresh your memories, we would take a trip down memory lane to remind you all of some of the horrible things you've had to say about me, just because you can:

'Oh, another brainless vapid celebrity spawn spending
    Daddy's money.'
'Looks good for a quick fumble. Then back to
    scrounging off Daddy.'
'She looks filthy.'
'I'd definitely use bleach before going near it.'
'No wonder she covers her face with her hair.'
'Large thighs!'
'She looks like a cocky little bitch.'
'She's too fugly to be a WAG, popstar, model. Y'know
    the usual things celebrities' kids do, so she's gone
    down the aspiring author route.'
'Lump of lard!'
'I would never have realised that was female.'
'Wondering, did she actually squeeze into that Ferrari
    or did Daddy have to shoehorn her in?'

'A bloated mess.'

'DROP DEAD.'

'She looks like a spoilt little bitch to me.'

'By the looks of her it seems she is waiting for food
parcels to arrive!'

'Hasn't worked a day in her life.'

'Another bleach blonde English with no class
pretending to be blonde!'

'Looks like Vicky Pollard.'

'Very smackable face in my opinion.'

'She needs to lose a lot of weight and go to make-up
college if she wants to become a celebrity!'

'She's a big lass!'

'Bit on the rough side isn't she?'

'Looks like she could throw a punch, just like her old
man. Common as . . .'

'Looks a right mutt.'

'Has Clarkson's daughter eaten Richard Hammond?'

'As my mum would say "a face only a mother could
love!"'

'Fatty boom boom alert.'

'I'm guessing JD Sports and Pizza Express deliver most
of her parcels.'

'She's a bit of a heffer.'

'Looks like she goes to Glastonbury, gets rattled
by fifteen lads n' doesn't even give her fanny a
onceover with a wet wipe.'

'She is ugly like her disgusting father.'

'Looks like a mean little witch!'

'Gobby Cow.'
'She's fat.'

And so it goes on. If I'm honest I had to stop there because, as thick-skinned as I'd like to think I am, there's only so many of these you can read before you want to lock yourself in a room and cry until you can't anymore, and I've got places to be and no more tears left to shed over you fuckers, so I thought I'd quit while I was ahead. And I know that this all sounds very 'look at me, look at me', which I know will earn me a whole new wave of criticism, but surely you have to see that this isn't *right*? That really, no one deserves this? That seventeen-year-old, insecure little me – who at this point had literally done no more to warrant this abuse than actually be alive – didn't deserve this? That I should have been allowed to carry my puppy fat in peace, and my grown-up fat for that matter, without the fear that one of you low-lifes was going to try and tear me down.

And you know what? I'm so far from a lone victim where all this is concerned. Internet trolling is something known, acknowledged and, more worryingly, accepted by the world right now to the point where it's pretty much just seen as one of those things – a 'well, darling, if you're going to *insist* on being like all of your friends and having a Facebook page then don't come crying to me when somebody tells you that you're so fat you should kill yourself. You chose Facebook, so you were kind of asking for it' kind of thing.

We've somehow got to the point where no one is safe online thanks to this freedom of expression – to the point where, compared to some of the things that are being shared, whether messages to 'celebrities' or people you actually know, what I've experienced is nothing; they're compliments by comparison. And that is disgusting.

Other than my weight, one of the biggest topics of conversation regarding my appearance that seems to pop up often is the size of my forehead. Apparently it's enormous. Apparently I look like an alien. I did always suspect this to be the case, if I'm honest. I don't remember a whole lot from my prep school days but one thing I do remember quite clearly was a guy in my class telling me I had a face that looked like a plate because my forehead was, and I quote, 'ginormous'. After saying this to me in Year 5 and giving me a life-long complex about the size of my head, I didn't see the guy again for years. Aged eighteen, however, I went to a friend's birthday party, a really fancy one in a nice part of London filled with parents, godparents and old teachers that this friend's parents were trying to impress. Anyway, there was my Year 5 tormentor, and he hardly even greeted me before grabbing me by the arm and asking me if I wanted to do cocaine with him. Unsurprisingly I declined class A drugs with a basic stranger and was met with this response: 'Oh, you're so fucking boring anyway. I always knew you'd grow up to be boring as fuck.' Blahblahblah.

It turns out this loser of a guy goes from acquaintance to acquaintance on a desperate hunt for cocaine under the illusion that drugs will make him interesting. Fuck knows what he's up to now but my money is NOT on him having started up a charity which gives money to the poor while coming home every night to a beautiful and kind girl who treats him well, who goes with him every other Sunday to visit his parents after a great dinner party the night before, full of friends who genuinely value him and his cooking. Nah, he'll be bouncing from job to job and girl to girl like he used to bounce from acquaintance to acquaintance, desperately confused as to why people aren't responding well to him when he tells them that their faces look like crockery.

To anyone currently being bullied at school and feeling that it will never end because the perpetrators will always be more powerful and more successful and more good-looking than you, you need to remember that people like this never grow up to be the people that you, or they, thought they would; trust me.)

Anyway, that complex has been stuck with me quite firmly since then, despite the fact that in between that knob-jockey pointing it out when I was ten, and then you fuckers reminding me when I turned seventeen, no one said anything about it to me. Quite simply because it would not have been a very nice thing to say. And *normal* people don't really like saying things that aren't very nice to each other. So why, I have to ask, do you people – who are probably passing off as normal-ish humans during the day, with jobs and dogs and homes and kids and bills – find yourselves scrolling through comments sections ready to blurt out the first nasty thing that pops into your head, just because you can? What makes you feel so high and mighty online, eh?

Let me show you some examples of what internet trolling might look like in the real world:

Lindsay: Oh my GOD, HI! You look amazing. It's been years, how are you? How are Jill and the kids? It's SO great to see you!

Troll: Your tits look like two pancakes sliding down a plate. There was a time when I would have bent you over and fucked fucked fucked you until I couldn't anymore but these days I wouldn't come near you with a bargepole.

Lindsay: Mark?! What? Why would you say that?

Troll: Oh, as if you didn't have it coming to you, you silly bitch, you've been whoring yourself out your whole life, always acting as if you were too good for everybody else and now you come crawling back wanting our attention, suddenly caring how Jill is? No one cares, you're so done.

Lindsay: I can't believe I'm hearing this, how I have been asking for it? Where is this coming from?

Troll: As if you don't know. Why not just go back to sucking dick, you filthy slapper? There's not a man alive who'd even come near you anymore.

★★★

Katie: Melissa, is that you? What a beautiful dress, I hardly recognised you!

Troll: I'm surprised you can see anything through all of that horrible make-up. Yes, it is me. You do realise that you look like a transvestite most days, don't you? It's not a good look, you know; you look like a dried-up old tart.

Katie: Oh thanks, say it how it really is, Melissa.

Troll: And another thing: am I the only one to notice that you actually look really old in person?

* * *

Tara: Guys, biggest news ever, I have a BOOK coming out!

Troll 1: Oh, you sucked off the publisher, did you?

Tara: What?! No!

Troll 2: Ahahaha, a book, that's laughable. You have to be the stupidest dumb bitch in the whole world, as if you could even write a book.

Tara: Wait, who are you?

Troll 3: Has anyone else noticed that her teeth are a kind of weird yellow colour?

Tara: * * Shuts her mouth* *

Troll 4: How many office chairs do you think were harmed by that fat arse in the making of this book?

Tara: * * Looks quickly to her bum* *

Troll 5: I would rather by stabbed in the neck every single day for the rest of my life than ever read something that this stupid cow has ever written.

Tara: Wait, that's horrible! Why?

Troll 6: I didn't even know this woman was still alive. #disappointed

Tara: * * Gulps* *

Troll 7: I reckon the instructions for my dishwasher would

make a more scintillating read than anything this
woman has to say.
Tara: Thanks.

***

Claire: Martin! It's so nice to see y—
Troll: GO THROW YOURSELF OFF A BRIDGE
YOU FUCKING C***.

This just doesn't happen in the real world! None of my
friends has ever called me fat, or commented on the size of
my forehead, or called me stupid or questioned my skill at
anything, apart from that one time I offered to make them
all dinner and only realised at 9 p.m. that I hadn't put the
oven on. Then my cooking ability was quite rightly called
into question, but the rest of the time they say nice things
to me, because, you know, it's quite nice to be nice. Or so I
thought.

Listen to these statistics found by the charity Ditch the
Label in 2013:

- Seven out of 10 young people have experienced
  cyberbullying.
- 37 per cent of young people have experienced
  cyberbullying on a 'highly frequent' basis.
- 20 per cent of young people have experienced
  'extreme cyberbullying' on a daily basis.

Of those:

- 62 per cent have been sent nasty private messages via smartphone apps.
- 47 per cent have received nasty profile comments.
- 40 per cent have received nasty photo comments.
- 42 per cent have received hate-based comments (racism, homophobia etc).
- 28 per cent have had personal information shared without consent.

And yet, despite all of these, 52 per cent have never reported the abuse they receive online and, of those that did report it, 26 per cent of them felt it wasn't taken seriously. And sorry, but four years have passed since these statistics were found. I dread to think what they must be now, as more and more of us spend more and more time glued to our mobile phones and stressing about our online presence.

I always thought you dwellers resided exclusively on Twitter, or in the comments sections of news articles, in places where you were all but a stranger to other people reading your poison. I assumed that trolling worked so well because it came about as a dangerous combination of anonymity and a complete lack of accountability, in that no one knows any more about you than whatever witty nickname you've decided to give yourself – the 140-character catchphrase that you have swiped from www. imafuckingdouchebagandwanttheworldtoknowitwhilst alsothinkingthatimsmartandfunny.com – and, judging by your chosen profile photo, that you have a cat you enjoy dressing up as pieces of fruit from time to time. I didn't think anyone actually had the balls to comment so nastily about another person when all their personal information, from their favourite colour to their star sign, was never further than a click away. But then I discovered evidence in the Ditch the Label study that young people are actually twice as likely to get bullied on Facebook than anywhere else.

And it really does beg some important questions: Why do you do this? What possesses you? Do you not think about the person on the other end of these comments? Or do you think about them to the point where you want to cause them pain? As far as comments to celebrities go, I suppose the assumption is that the likes of Lindsay Lohan and Kim Kardashian are not going to spend their evenings scrolling through the comments section to see what you all had to say about them. I suppose the assumption is that they will never see what you have to say and that you are just saying these things because you can. You're saying them *about* them, rather than *to* them, so it doesn't really count, it doesn't cause any harm. It doesn't *matter*. That assumption, I'm afraid, is wrong, for two main reasons:

1. Celebrities do read the comments. They shouldn't, they know they shouldn't, but it's hard not to, right? I'm obviously not a celebrity in any capacity, but when strangers make comments about my appearance, as we have established that they like to

do, I can't help but look. When there are comments
on Instagram posts I quite obviously want to see
them, much as I would if a friend commented on a
photo on my private Facebook page. When people
say things about us, or write things about us, we
want to know what they're saying; it's human nature.
And so while the likes of Kylie Jenner might not
make it through the 400,000 comments all the way
to yours, they will see enough of them to get the gist
of it, and sadly the negative comments will stay with
them for much much longer than the nice ones will,
because that is also human nature, and celebrities are
human beings too, remember.

2. The comments are dangerous because of the
   other people reading them. OK, so let's say that
   Ariel Winter puts up a photograph of herself in
   a bikini on Instagram and the photo does the
   rounds through the *Daily Mail* sidebar of shame
   and then onto Facebook pages and Twitter feeds.
   She realistically will not get a chance to read every
   single comment that comes in on every single
   platform. But that's not to say that the comments
   won't get seen by lots of other unsuspecting eyes.
   Ariel Winter has a beautiful, very enviable figure
   but, because we are in 2017 and everyone is a dick,
   there are lots of people out there who are willing,
   despite her tender age, to tear her to shreds for
   being 'fat' etc. etc. Now what worries me is that
   the world is full of people who are much bigger

than Ariel, most of them not nearly as confident.
So how do you suppose it makes them feel when
they see photos of Ariel Winter, looking incredible
and beautiful and seemingly a million miles from
anything they could hope to look like, being called
'obese' and 'ugly' and that she is going to die of
diabetes unless she stops eating so much? How
do you think it feels for girls who are aspiring to
someone who is then being told *they* are too fat?
How shattered are they going to feel?

The thing that we, well you, really NEED to remember
is that your words do hurt. And as with all things in life,
your actions do have consequences. Catastrophic ones in
some instances. According to the Pew Research Center
Internet Project, 2011, 95 per cent of teenagers are online.
The Cyberbullying Hotline found that 42 per cent of all
teenagers have reported being cyberbullied over the past
year, with one in five thinking about suicide and one in
ten attempting it. So, this means in an average classroom
of thirty teens, twenty-eight are online, twelve have been
cyberbullied, three have thought about SUICIDE and one
has actually attempted it because they've been made to feel
SO unhappy by people who are at best disguised as normal
people, and at worst disguised as their friends.

That's a member of a family, a child, who should have
a beautifully optimistic view of the world but instead has
been driven to suicide attempts by a society that sees online
trolling as *one of those things*. Kids are so used to it now that,

when asked, 81 per cent of teenagers said simply that it was easier to get away with bullying online.

And that is a conversation in itself. Why is it so easy to bully online? Well, the answer is three-fold, I think. The first thing to take into consideration is that there is of course no real accountability online; you can basically say anything you want and get away with it because no one knows for certain who you are if you don't want them to. The second thing is this: since social media is so new, few of today's children's parents know the first thing about it. Since kids now know how their parents' iPads work better than they do, mums and dads probably don't feel they have a great position of authority when it comes to implementing rules on Facebook and Twitter, if they know that rules need implementing at all. They're probably still advising their children that it's wrong to tease, that they shouldn't pull hair or steal dinner money in the playground (assuming money is still being used and all of these kids aren't just using ApplePay), but they say nothing about 'fraping', or trolling, or slut-shaming online. Because they don't know what they CAN say.

And then there are the kids themselves, the ones that are probably nice enough children, from nice enough families, who for some reason turn into evil little shits online. Why do they do that? Well, for the same reasons that an old-fashioned bully bullies, I suppose. Because they feel they need to, because they have been bullied and they feel that the best defence is a good offence, maybe. Perhaps it's that, or perhaps it's because they are to a degree encouraged to do it – encouraged by the article that just popped up on Facebook or in the paper that their mummy was reading that morning, the one in which the journalist was shaming a woman for not wearing enough make-up or gaining weight. Personally, I think it's a combination of all these things. The same nasty shit that's always happened – just on a bigger stage, to a more accepting audience. And that's a worry in its own right.

When I talk to friends about the abuse I receive online they're shocked. They tell me that you're all arseholes, that you're the scum of the earth and tragic and pathetic and I shouldn't waste my time caring about you. They tell me that you act out of jealousy and you cannot be taken seriously because you are nothing more than small low-lifes that will achieve nothing of note with your lives – much like the guy who used to ridicule me for my alien head. But what they don't understand, what they can't understand, is how much your words hurt. How much it hurts to have someone, to all intents and purposes, justifying your insecurities, basically vocalising the voice in your head that says 'you're too fat', 'your teeth aren't white enough', 'your head looks like a kitchen appliance'.

All the things I'm self-conscious about are, all of a sudden, legitimate things that I have every right to be embarrassed about, because they are actually noticeable problems that other people can see and that don't, like I'd hoped, just live in my reflection. I have now developed a very thick skin, thankfully. But I'm pissed off that I had to; that this is such an accepted part of being in the public eye. Hell, that it's an accepted part of being alive; that we live in a culture that assumes if one finds themselves in a position of success and fame that they must automatically brace themselves for all of the abuse they now somehow *deserve*.

I'm pissed off that when I typed 'cyberbullying' into Google, the next words that appeared as a suggestion were 'depression' and 'suicide'. That despite the fact that the stories we're seeing more and more of in the news at the moment – of young people, still at school, killing themselves because of messages they've received online – people are still prepared to push their peers to that level of despair. I'm pissed off that cyberbullying is so prevalent. That it is a *thing* at all. That hurting people to their faces isn't enough anymore; that we're so sure we're right, that our view is so important, that the world can't possibly live without just one more nugget of wisdom from our brains, so we NEED to give the people what they want, and that ultimately we are so cowardly that this all happens from the safety of not just your mothers' basements up and down the country, but under desks in classrooms and on the shared family computer. (Are they even a thing anymore or does everyone legally need their own laptop or tablet now?) That we have got to the point where these thoughts are so close to the surface that they're just behind the lips of nearly every person you see; that the actions are so cruel and so normal in equal measure that they strip our new world of kindness and trust before it even has the chance to show us greatness. I hate everything you are and I hate the world you're creating. I hate what we are becoming, not least because social media isn't going anywhere anytime soon.

But I can't leave you with that, at risk of letting you think you've won before the battle has even really started so, instead, I will leave you with this: after the last particularly shitty batch of comments that came through about me something wonderful did happen – one friend stopped by with a bunch of roses to give me a big cuddle and tell me that I didn't deserve this and another friend even posted me a cake, from 100 miles away, that was both gluten- and dairy-free, with the words 'You Are Beautiful' written on top of it. Which at least proved this to me: you will never win, because kindness will always shine through much brighter. The victim of your abuse is loved in ways you can't understand and, so long as they can remember that, and never lose sight of the light, then you are powerless. But until the day that all of your power is stripped, I must ask you this: if the words that you spoke were written on your skin, would you still be beautiful?

I didn't think so.

Em

Dear No More Page 3 Campaigners

Hiya guys. How are you? I know you don't particularly like me, and I know we've had our differences in the past, but I just wanted to get in touch as a fellow woman to see if I can make head or tail of your debate and chat through, in a calm manner, where I'm at with all of this. I don't want to shout and scream and be unreasonable; fundamentally I know we're not *that* different underneath all of this, so here goes …

Last time we spoke, in November 2014, you were on the cusp of winning your battle to get breasts out of the *Sun*. Congratulations on your success. I don't love it, I'm not happy about it, but congratulations nonetheless – you campaigned tirelessly and I take my hat off to you.

So, first things first, in case you couldn't tell, you ought to know that I LOVE Page 3; well, I loved it. Not because I'm a creeper or a nudist and not because I like staring at topless women particularly, but because I thought it was great.

I loved it that after however many umpteen years, women had actually earned the right to take their kit off and pose in a national newspaper. I loved that these girls were smiling. I loved that they were strong and independent and were their own women. I loved that they were curvy. I loved that they were topless. You, on the other hand, did not. You thought it was degrading, that they were being objectified, and that a national newspaper – where there is a risk that children could see it – was not the place for that sort of thing. Which I understand, of course. We don't necessarily want to be exposing our children to nudity at a young age if we can avoid it. I'd probably be arguing the same thing, if I thought that it could be avoided at all . . .

But by my reckoning this can't be avoided. Kids now, thanks to advancements in technology and the world's obsession with social media, are seeing far, far worse than a nipple in a newspaper. Hell, they're seeing far worse just by scrolling through their Facebook newsfeed. After they've trawled their way through images of war-torn Syria, videos of ISIS beheading prisoners and blurry footage of politicians snorting cocaine off every flat surface they can find while degrading a hooker, they are then encouraged, sometimes even by their parents, who are aware that the internet is full of nastiness, to turn to the likes of Miley Cyrus for a bit of light relief, some entertainment. Only then to find out of course that Miley Cyrus, despite having been a 'Disney star, child-friendly, before-the-watershed' fun role model, is now actually like Page 3 on acid. And it's the same story everywhere. If they're not being bombarded by terrifying images of the state of the world, then it's skirts too short, heels too high, cleavage too much on the bodies of their role models.

Even Little Mix, adored by millions of young girls,

wear next to nothing to perform. Rihanna/Katy Perry/
Madonna – all of them 'sex symbols'. Kids can't open their
eyes anymore without seeing something *inappropriate* and,
try as we might to control that, there is actually sweet fuck
all we can do about it. So part of me thought: why are you
bothering fighting one nipple in one newspaper when artists
like Robin Thicke are making incredibly popular music
videos full of girls rubbing themselves on things like dogs
with worms? The other part of me thought: if we accept
that kids are going to see nudity wherever they go anyway,
wouldn't I rather it be controlled, in the house, on Page 3 of
my newspaper where I can talk it through with them? Still
now, the more I think about it, the more I think that, given
the times, Page 3 was a good thing and one we could do
with having back.

My only concern that ever came from children seeing
Page 3 was that these women were not a fair representation
of size 16 Britain. I didn't want prepubescent girls looking
at photos of these women and thinking: why don't I look
like that? Nor did I want overweight girls looking at images
of beaming size 8s/10s/12s and thinking: no one will find
me attractive if I don't lose weight and get my tits done. But
then I had a closer look and realised that not one of these
girls was 'thin' anyway, and that Lucy Vixen is at least a size
14 now, and I realised that actually made a refreshing change
from the rest of the nearly naked women we see every day
(here's looking at Miley again).

I think it's actually rather lovely to have a woman with
hips AND tits so happy to display herself. It's also swell that

she's smiling rather than giving us that strange blowjob pout that we've become so used to seeing. With this in mind I can honestly say that I would rather my children studied Page 3 every day for the rest of their lives than watched anything on MTV.

The fact of the matter is from the minute we are born we see breasts. Hell, for the first year of their lives even little boys, who will never grow up to have any themselves, are literally sucking on one. They then get older and their mates start showing them photos they found in their dads' desk drawers (I'm a 1990s baby, so this probably doesn't happen anymore). Then they get access to an iPhone and find photos and videos on the internet. Then, when they turn on the TV, rest assured there'll be some scantily clad woman shaking her ass in the direction of the camera. Then they'll walk through a shop and see rows of photos on the covers of endless magazines and newspapers of Rihanna's 'nip slip' and then, one day, when they're very lucky, they will court a woman until she is, in turn, ready to show him her nipples, and one day he might be fortunate enough to see his son or daughter feeding from his wife's breasts.

When you think about it like that, is Page 3 still the crisis you're making it out to be? Or is it maybe, and bear with me here, a good thing? Working on the logic that everywhere we look we're exposed to nudity in some shape or form, isn't it sort of fabulous that by having it on the first double-spread of the country's most popular newspaper, we're normalising it? We're removing the stigma around a nipple so that when young boys become teenage boys they're not obsessing over the most natural thing in the world as if it were forbidden fruit. Rather, they accept it as a totally normal part of being a woman. That, just like them, women have nipples they aren't forced into hiding? It might also mean that when they do meet a woman willing to take her top off for them, they're not shocked and disgusted to find out she measures more than twenty inches around the waist.

Because this is the other thing that annoys me, and if you remember correctly, the argument I came to you with last time our paths crossed. 'Feminists' criticise Page 3 every day and yet when an actress takes her kit off, in black and white of course, for an 'artistic' shoot, the same people celebrate her for her bravery and beauty. This happened when Keira Knightley took off her clothes for a shoot with *Interview* magazine. She was applauded for doing THE VERY SAME THING that Page 3 girls got stick for every day. It happened again earlier this year when Emma Watson posed topless for the front cover of *Elle*.

The response was overwhelmingly good; she was applauded for her bravery and told she was inspiring and beautiful. This left me fuming, not because she isn't inspiring and beautiful, but on account of the huge injustice here. What makes the two things different in any way? The fact that when Keira and Emma posed for their photos it was under the pretence of art? Or, more worryingly, is it a class thing? Worse still, is it because of their sizes, because both Keira and Emma are thin? I don't know, but I do know that if you don't like one then you can't celebrate the other. You

can't #freethenipple or 'share' Keira's images all the while
arguing that the national press isn't the place for boobies, that
you're worried about exposing your children to too much. I
mean, for Godssake, Emma Watson did the *Elle* shoot as part
of the publicity for *Beauty and the Beast*, the recent Disney
film she acted in. To applaud a Disney princess posing naked
and criticise an honest girl from Bedford trying to make a
go of it as a model is ridiculous, and hypocrisy at its finest.
You're either for women taking their clothes off for a print
publication, or you're against it.

One of your other biggest concerns, as I understand it, is
that Page 3 encourages men to see women as objects. But I
feel the need to dispute this, because when it comes to this
sort of thing I think that Page 3 is the least of our worries.

I AM a feminist. A die-hard. I believe that women
should be equal to men, end of story, so please don't call
that into question as I continue, but there are SO many
problems facing women every day and I just don't consider
Page 3 to be one of them. Of course I won't deny that
women are objectified, it happens all the flipping time,
but let's look at the facts here. Objectification happens for
a whole load of reasons: poor education, poor role models,
exposure to pornography, peer pressure. The fact that
women are objectified is due to a fundamental problem
in our society and not, to my mind, as a direct result of a
man seeing a topless woman in the paper. Yes, I understand
that when Dave looks up from his paper and sees a girl
with big 'knockers' walking past his van window, he may
be encouraged to holler at her, mistakenly believing she is

in some way 'asking for it', but do you think he REALLY did that because the newspaper told him to? Do you think before he read it he was quiet and calm and nice and polite and respectful? Or do you think perhaps that Dave always had it in him and that had he been educated and taught more respect and better manners this could be prevented? And most importantly, did you assume that after Page 3 got removed that the likes of Dave would suddenly realise what sexist pigs they had been and stop? Not a chance in hell. For whatever reason, Dave and his mates feel they have the right to do this. They did it before Page 3 and they've done it since. There is a problem here but Page 3 isn't the root cause.

I love what you are TRYING to do. I so admire your passion and your drive and, underneath all of this booby bollocks, I love your message. I love that on the back of your 2014 victory you have turned your attention to sexism in the media on a wider level. Because that is really important. The shitty journalists all clamouring for a photograph of a celeb (even if no one has ever heard of them) in a bikini, all the while planning whatever ridiculous body-shaming headline they've already used twelve times that day to accompany it, are the problem. THIS is where a large part of the objectification of women originates. A long-lensed camera sneaking through the railings of Angelina Jolie's hotel compound to take a photo of her in her pants, while Brad Pitt stands waving his willy around in the next door room is ignored – that is objectification of women. A girl standing naked because she wants to on Page 3, dare I say it, might even be empowerment.

Because men are no longer, in my opinion, these horny, uncontrollable sex pests we make them out to be. Many of the Page 3 girls now have massive followings on their Instagram accounts and, if you scroll through the comments section, the 'I want to wank over you' comments are fewer and farther between these days, replaced with 'Wow, you're so beautiful' ones en masse. Go see for yourselves. I regularly see vigilantes (always men) calling out the misogynistic pigs who blab on about their erections. And some of the nastiest comments? Well, they're coming from women.

Take Lacey Banghard, a former Page 3 girl and friend of mine – she's now running her own business and smashing life. The *Sun* offered her a last shoot with them (in which she wore a suit) where they interviewed her about her career and investments. Her Instagram is brimming with support from men who are inspired and in awe of her; yes, they went there initially because of her 'assets' but they stuck around because she's cool. She's empowering. It's the same story with another friend and former Page 3 girl Peta Todd, who since quitting modelling now has a weekly column in the *Sun*, is a patron for *Help for Heroes* AND an amazing mother to three children. Again, her following is still huge and she is still loved because she is in her own right a truly amazing woman. Of all the women I know, these are two of the most inspirational . . . what does that tell you?

'News in Briefs', you have to remember, was a tongue-in-cheek idea, meant to be funny. And now, after seeing the success of people like Lacey, I do wonder whether if by assuming that all these women are good for is being objectified you're the ones causing the problems here. I don't know why you had to go all guns blazing for Page 3 when there are so many other elements of the media requiring your attention. If I was given the choice of letting my kids see nipples on curvy women all day every day or teeny tiny skinny women dancing provocatively, I'd go for the nipples every time.

Look, I really do love how you are asking for 'equal representation in our news media, by relentlessly drawing attention to the sublime, the ridiculous and the sometimes downright dangerous' because this is what I do too; we have this in common. There is a lot out there that is truly worrying and dangerous, but what you don't seem to understand is that Page 3 is not, in the grand scheme of things, the enemy.

When I was younger I read *Heat* magazine religiously, and have spent time drooling over their Torso of the Month. Was I sexist for that? Was I objectifying this celebrity? Should I not have seen it as a teenager? Is this the next battle, getting those banned? What about the calendar my mum bought me for Christmas of the naked Royal Marines – am I playing a part in the objectification of men by having it up on my wall? No wait, I can't be, because we're not equal yet, are we?

I wish you all the luck in the world with your future ventures. I hope that one day we do have equality in the newspapers and that women will not be objectified at every turn. But I also hope, with all of my heart, that one day I will see a boob in a newspaper again, perhaps alongside the brand new Page 2, a page dedicated to naked men? Maybe we could work together for that?

Here's hoping,

Em

Dear The Sidebar Of Shame

cc Daily Mail *journalists, editors, photographers*

When I was younger, the only publication I ever actually read, other than *Dear Deirdre* in the *Sun* and the *Funday Times*, was *Heat* magazine. This was before the days of online everything, so in order to stay abreast of all things current (and by that I mean 'who is shagging who?'), I would spend my pocket money on it or wait until grown-ups I knew read it were done with it and beg them to pass it on to me.

I never watched a huge amount of reality TV and didn't actually have any celebrities I aspired to or 'fan-girled' over in a huge way, unless you count Avril Lavigne circa 2004, but for some reason I frigging loved that magazine. At the time, as a young teenager, I never saw a problem with it. I suspect I was at an age where I understood very little about celebrity culture and, as a result, I probably believed that if you were in the public eye then you belonged to the masses. Being the daughter of a celebrity didn't help sway me to believe otherwise; for as long as I could remember, various details of our family life were common knowledge; our address was on Google. If I went out with my dad people would stop to take pictures, and if we ever went to a swanky event, we were expected to wait on the red carpet to have our photos taken.

What happened to all of those photos? At the time I didn't know or really care and since we never appeared in the pages of *Heat* it never occurred to me that they would be used for anything, I just thought it was one of those things that came with having a father in the limelight. (There was a point where I naïvely thought they were just taken for us!)

When I was about ten, we went to see *Mary Poppins* at the theatre and a really sweet family photo was taken by a photographer and sent to us. We framed it and it still lives in the sitting room; why would anyone else want that picture? I thought. It's not their family!

As I got older, though, I began to hate the press – more specifically the 'showbiz' articles relentlessly appearing on the sidebar of the MailOnline website and, I realise now, in the pages of the magazines I adored so much. I began to notice that the family photos we had posed for so innocently would one day be dragged up to use in a smear piece; that all of a sudden it was a bit more sinister and intense than just a case of having our address on Google. Our secrets were common knowledge and, really, all these articles were – all they had ever been – were invitations for people to judge us. Judge us on what we looked like, what we wore and what we did.

But before all of this, before I knew how evil all of this really was, I really did love *Heat* magazine. My mother on the other hand HATED it. She hated that I read it and would regularly make comments about what gutter press it was. At the time I had perfectly perfected my teenage

eye-roll, and of course assumed that any comment made
about anything I had shown any interest in at all was by its
very definition a personal attack on me. I would find myself
getting very defensive of this publication, assuming that
the reason my mum didn't like it was because she was *old,*
because she hadn't heard of anyone, because she just didn't
get it. That magazine was my one connection to adult life;
my one access point into the glitz and glam I so longed to be
a part of.

I would look at photos of Katie Price's fairytale wedding,
watch from afar as Britney Spears had the most public
meltdown in human history – which was documented and
published for all the world to see – and I would take some
sick pleasure in turning to the double-spread that was the
'circle of shame' section: pages used exclusively to shame
celebrities. Tit-tape on show? Circled. Forgot to shave your
armpits? Circled. Flashed your pants? Circled. Boob job scar
visible? Circled. Back fat? Circled. Smudged your make-up?
Circled. Lipstick on your teeth? Circled. If you are spotted
looking anything other than perfect? Well, I just hope you're
ready to land on the desk of some hack with highlighter
in her hand and a chip on her shoulder. Did it occur to me
at the time that women being shamed for the flimsiest of
reasons would contribute so heavily to the insecurities about
to come as I grew up? Nope. Did I notice the blatant sexism?
The fact that all these images were of women and not once
did I see a man being circled for doing anything? Again,
no I didn't. Did I hear it when in 2003 Ewan McGregor
described *Heat* as a 'dirty, filthy piece of shit' over the use of

its paparazzi photos. Of course not. At the time I thought this was just mild entertainment, something I had the right to enjoy.

I don't remember it, but subsequent research has shown me that in 2007 – when I was twelve years old and *Heat* magazine was at its most interesting to me – they included a tasteless sticker with the slogan 'Harvey Wants To Eat Me' as part of a cruel article about Katie Price's disabled son. Although the publication apologised afterwards and made a donation to charity, as Editor Lucie Cave told the Leveson Inquiry: 'It was a grave mistake. Everyone who worked for the magazine at the time and still works for the magazine is mortified by that incident.'

You do find yourself wondering, why did they do it in the first place? Because they thought they could. This was sick journalism at its most cynical, but was really nothing of what was to come.

Despite what Lucie Cave said in an interview in 2013 about not fearing the *Daily Mail* following the dramatic decline of magazine sales, it doesn't take a genius to work out that as your Sidebar of Shame grew in popularity, sales of the magazine doing the same thing in slow-motion were bound to fall. I was the perfect example of this. When I left school and moved to London aged eighteen I stopped buying magazines altogether and would spend my lunchbreaks scoffing tuna mayo baguettes and chocolate brownies, completely missing the irony that, as I stuffed my face with calorie upon calorie, hating my ever-growing waistline and hiding under ever-thicker jumpers, I was taking sweet, sick satisfaction in watching celebrities being shamed for gaining weight, wearing the wrong dress or neglecting to wash their hair. I LOVED that there were new stories every day, hell, every hour. It was like *Heat* had whet my appetite and the *Daily Mail* was the all-you-can-eat buffet I'd gained access to after years of collecting coupons. I loved that these stories were never-ending, that if I was ever bored at work, the carnage that was planet celebrity was never more than a click away. I loved it, until I became a target of it.

The first time I saw a photo of myself in the *Daily Mail* I was seventeen. It was the day of my Leavers' Ball (no, I am NOT going to call it a prom) and, lastminute.com as ever, Dad and I had neglected to buy a dress until the very final moment A.K.A. that afternoon. It was a big rite of passage for us for some reason, his eldest daughter leaving school, and we decided to make a day of it. We went first to the dress shop and, in the afternoon, to a café in west London where we sat and drank coffee and smoked cigarettes. (Am I proud of my teen addiction? Nope. Is it any of your business? Nope.) We then got in the car to go back to my school for the party. What I didn't know was that the entire time we were in the café someone was taking photos of us. I only spotted him as I was getting back into the passenger seat of a Ferrari that QUITE OBVIOUSLY WASN'T MINE and I turned to look at him (something I will regret forever) and was captured pulling a 'silly face'.

I didn't think anything more about it until the next day. Which was my first day of freedom. My first day as an adult, my first day out all alone in the big wide world. The day I

realised that, unless I toughened up quick sticks, my life was
about to become painstakingly shit. For there I was, in all
my glory, on the Sidebar of Shame: 'Just your average day
out with Dad! Jeremy Clarkson takes his teenage daughter
for a spin in his red Ferrari'. And there it began. I'm no Kim
K, obvi not, but from time to time I'll be scrolling through
the *Daily Mail*, these days mostly looking for inspiration for
blog articles, and I'll see myself, that same stupid face (why
do you INSIST on using that horrible six-year-old photo of
me?) gawping out at me.

And so it has gone on. From time to time someone will
pick up on a tweet, I'll be seen out in public with my dad,
or I'll be quizzed over my 'bikini body'. (Which, just for
your notes, is EXACTLY THE SAME AS MY NORMAL
BODY except for instead of covering it with jeans and
jumpers, required on the cold streets of London, I put on
smaller pieces of fabric that are more appropriate for sunnier
climates. Exactly the same body, different things on it . . . do
you understand?)

There is so much more I want to talk about that I'm hard
pushed finding a place to start. I suppose the obvious place
would be at the beginning, the thing that entices us to read
all this shite in the first place, and that would be with the
headline. I am rather conveniently writing this letter on
Halloween and your sidebar is awash with images of women,
dare I even say it, out having fun. Let's see what constituted
news today, shall we? (On a day when the migrant crisis is at
its peak and the US presidential elections are only eight days
away.) Let's see quite how much 'slut-shaming' journalism

you guys managed to squeeze into this relatively small space? (Translation included to highlight quite how ridiculous you have all become.)

'Chloe Ferry almost spills out of her skimpy Halloween outfit as she stumbles out of club during wild night out in Newcastle'
Translation: *Geordie Shore* star falls over

'Hilton teams a flirty Superwoman costume with racy thigh-high boots as she parties up a storm at Halloween bash'
Translation: Paris Hilton dressed up as Superwoman

'Models Hailey Clauson and Ashley Smith wear little clothing for Halloween bash'
Translation: Models go out

'Lauren Silverman suffers embarrassing wardrobe malfunction as she exposes too much in racy lace top after *The X Factor*'
Translation: Pestering pap couldn't believe his luck

'Christina Aguilera wows fans with a VERY raunchy video to her newly remixed version of *The Get Down* soundtrack "Telepathy"'
Translation: Christina Aguilera has a new single out

'Scantily clad Charli XCX releases raunchy

Halloween-inspired music video to latest hit "After the
Afterparty"'
Translation: Charli XCX has a new single out

'Joanna Krupa unleashes her inner Aphrodite in a risqué
Greek goddess outfit at Halloween bash as she dons
THIRD costume in as many days'
Translation: Joanna Kruppa gets invited to a lot of parties

'Lindsay Lohan posts a very racy snap of herself wearing
sexy hot pink lingerie as she celebrates Halloween'
Translation: Lindsay Lohan took a selfie

'Bella Hadid goes braless in skintight plunging denim
jumpsuit at Victoria's Secret fashion show fitting'
Translation: Bella Hadid goes to work.

'Denise Welch, 58, shows off her curves in a blue lace
gown to support husband Lincoln Townley, 43, at the
BAFTA Britannia Awards in Beverly Hills'
Translation: Denise Welch went to the BAFTA Britannia
Awards
(Please note that no one young had their ages
mentioned)

'Gwen Stefani shows off her toned tummy in punky
tartan trousers and a floral top at stadium show in
California'
Translation: Gwen Stefani did her job

'Jennifer Garner goes make-up free as she braves the wet weather for low-key day out with her children'
Translation: Jennifer Garner went outside

And so it goes on, and on, and on.

You guys are unreal, each of you like a little walking, talking thesaurus. Each description more ridiculous than the last. I often find myself wondering if THIS is the fundamental difference between men and women. Where a man can wear whatever he wants and go wherever he pleases, a woman is left constantly 'struggling' and 'falling' – whether that's describing the journey or her outfit, I am often unsure, but the difference IS remarkable. I have however, finally mastered the basics:

Busty: has worn a low-cut top.
Leggy display: has worn a short skirt.
Scantily clad: hasn't worn a lot.
Curvaceous: isn't thin enough.
Fuller figure: is fat.
Wardrobe malfunction: outfit no longer perfect.
Little to the imagination: top is probably a bit see-through.
Flaunts her figure: wears a dress.
Looks all grown up: is finally legal.

So I get it now, and I hate it more than ever. Surely this is a shocking waste of a journalist's talents?! Are you proud of yourselves for your articles? Are your careers really all you ever hoped and dreamed they would be as you slogged over textbooks accumulating thousands of pounds' worth of debt in order to master this tricky trade? Do you ring your mother every time you get published to show off how you were the first to write about Kim Kardashian's new shoes? Do you frame them? Are you really happy this is what your lives have become? Because, no disrespect here, this is a shambles.

It has been widely reported that the most amount of money ever offered to a pap was $4.1 million for the first photo of Brangelina's (RIP dream couple) first baby together – there used to be good money in that industry. An industry I have grown to despise but one I now realise was vital to the likes of Paris Hilton, who relied entirely on these scumbags to make a name for themselves. But now? Now there's a pap on every corner waiting to watch the Kardashian clan buy a smoothie and all of Britain's homegrown reality TV stars have their numbers on speed dial.

You then take into consideration that over a half of the Sidebar of Shame is now made up of Instagram photos and Snapchat stories and you realise quite quickly that this is an incredibly oversaturated market. There are more 'celebrities' now than there have ever been because, thanks to publications like this one, all a girl need really do these days to get her five minutes is take the bins out in her pants. She then hires the right PR team and she's got that five-minute slot every morning, as regular as Jeremy Kyle. And you poor fuckers are left to write the same mindless drivel day in, day out. If I wasn't so disappointed and angry with the whole thing, I'd almost feel sorry for you.

I don't know what it is that keeps bringing me back to you, and I actually worry that it's the sick fascination that I, along with the 24 million other readers that make up your net readership, seem to have with this aspect of humankind that results in you being the most-read online newspaper in the UK. While your shoddy journalism is laughable at times, your studies that find EVERYTHING is going to give us cancer are downright ridiculous, and that to the masses – the smart, normal, decent masses – your newspaper is not considered a serious publication, the worrying fact is this: people love you. For whatever reason you're not just a guilty pleasure anymore, you're a full-blown addiction to so many of us.

The day that Theresa May got the keys to Downing Street after replacing David Cameron as Prime Minister in 2016, the *Metro* ran with the headline: 'Theresa May's husband steals the show in sexy navy suit as he starts new life as First Man'. The story went on to explain, in a fabulously sarcastic way, every inch of his outfit, completely omitting any mention of his successful career, in a clear jab at the journalism we have come to expect from some publications. (It was a clear jab at you and your publication.) Because everyone knows there is nothing more important in your eyes than a woman's outfit.

Samantha Cameron, despite having a flourishing career in her own right as Creative Director of Smythson, was never, ever, more than a mannequin to you. The world is

chock-a-block with women doing incredible things, and
yet, if you can't tell us where her coat is from then it's not
really an article worth writing, is it? Emma Watson, Lena
Dunham, Kate Middleton, Angelina Jolie – all successful
women doing properly impressive things – and STILL you
can be sure that the headline will make reference to their
outfits or their figures.

As we have established, unattractive female celebrities just
don't cut the mustard; even if the beauty ideals did somehow
let them slip through their horrible fingers, you won't let
them. If they're overweight at the beginning of their careers,
rest assured they cut carbs out immediately. If they dress
badly, by the end of their first week they'll have a personal
shopper. If their face is anything other than perfect, well,
they'll either hire the best make-up artist money can buy
or it's off to the clinic for a quick procedure. It's a horrible
culture, it's fake and it's nasty, and I don't for a minute
imagine that these women like living like that. So why do
we think they do it? Well, they do it because they have to . . .
even me who has been 'papped' less than ten times in my
entire life finds myself thinking twice as hard about what I'm
wearing if I know I'll be meeting my dad in public, and I
get properly frightened of my own bad hair days. I genuinely
can't imagine what it must be like for those people to whom
it happens every day and who are, in your eyes at least,
nothing more than professionally pretty.

They do it, they do all of it, because YOU make them.
You drive them to it. You will shame the living shit out of
them until they make the change. But what annoys me the

most about all of this is that you're doing this from behind a computer screen. You're as bad as the trolls; you are cowards, hiding in big offices, silently digging into these women until there's nowhere left to dig. And you're doing it as your job. You're doing it on days when you have a cold and look awful and exhausted. On days when you have forgotten to wash your hair. On days when you're hungover and you've eaten fifteen muffins. On days when your cat died and you're sad. On days when you just couldn't be arsed to make an effort. And you sit there, an over-indulged, dirty, snotty mess, and you deem other women to be not good enough.

You are part of the majority that sits on the beach on holiday with your arms folded across your stomach because you're painfully aware that you ate too much at lunch and you don't like your stomach rolls. You are part of the majority that got changed twelve times before going to a party because everything you owned clung in horrible ways to your stomach. You are part of the majority that spends a lot of time looking at themselves in the mirror and finding so much wrong with your face. All because society is telling you that YOU aren't good enough. But where does society learn these things, I have to ask? Why, the media of course. They take their lead from you.

So not only are you victims of your own success, but you are tearing the rest of us down with you. We are now ALL victims of your success. And we've got to stop this.

We all know that a woman is worth more than her outfit, that she can be beautiful at any size and that ultimately it's what's on the inside that counts. But you are making it incredibly difficult for us to maintain faith in that. You are sharing these stories on such a massive platform that those good, honest, unsuspecting visitors to your site – who are there to find out if it's true that looking at a tree for too long in autumn can give you cancer – are subject to sexism in its rawest form. And they are invited to judge; they're literally begged to do it. And so they do, because they can't help themselves, because just like you and me they are humans too. And before you know it they're on the bus on the way home shooting nasty looks left, right and centre because if Lauren Goodger is considered fat then Jesus Christ everyone on this commute is enormous. They'll get home and look in the mirror and realise they're a way off having a perfect nose and, before you can say Harley Street, there's another cadet in the ranks of insecurity, just because they saw a photo of a chick in her knickers on the right-hand side of some website and clicked through.

Despite everything I consider myself fairly lucky. I was of an age where, when I was at my most vulnerable, the *Daily Mail* did not yet exist in my consciousness, and I had to settle for my regular instalments from *Heat*. But now? Twenty-first century babes are getting this hateful propaganda on the hour every hour. They don't just see it in the magazine racks at the shops anymore; they see it on their Facebook pages, on their kitchen tables, on their Instagram accounts, on Twitter. They see it EVERYWHERE. Does that not scare you, the fact that they cannot get away from it? Because it terrifies me.

Surely this is enough now, guys. You write for the most

popular newspaper in the country, so before you pen your next piece please ask yourself if you'd genuinely be cool letting your daughters read this stuff every single day. Because mine are going to get the same response from me if they read it as I did from my mum, as I poured over *Heat*. Unless of course I've found a way to block it from appearing on their computers in any capacity before they're old enough to realise – because I can't and I won't expose them to something that is just so cruel and hateful.

Please make this right, before it really is too late.

Thanks,

Em

P.S. Please, please, block that comments section of yours. Your readers are not only not intelligent, they're mean, and you're evoking a response in them that is causing all sorts of different issues. See the letter that I sent to online trolls? I'll cc you in.

Dear Mum

OK, I know this will make you cry so I'll keep it short, but I had to write you a little letter. I'm sorry that you didn't see this before the book was published but I know you're much too modest and self-deprecating and would have made me take it out, so I hope you understand why I've had to do it like this! I need to start by saying thank you. Thank you so much for everything. From the very first day of my life you have been there for me, you've spoilt me rotten, you've taken so much shit, you've been the most supportive and amazing role model to me and I know that I have been luckier than most to have such a special relationship with you.

Whenever people ask me who my hero is in life, I always say 'my mum'. I've never even had to think about it. There are lots of phenomenal women out there, and I admire so many of them so much, but none in the way that I look up to you.

I took you for granted for the first eighteen years of my life and I need to say that I'm sorry for doing that. I was teenage and angsty and difficult and it was so easy to take it out on you. You'd tell me not to do things and be angry with me for getting my nose pierced or not tidying my bedroom, and I would be SO furious with you for being *so like, totally unfair.* You'd take me shopping and nothing would fit me and, because you were there, you'd be the one who would bear the brunt of my frustration. I'd come home from school having had a shitty day and I'd take it all out on you because you were the person standing right in front of me. I'd have fights with my friends and somehow it would become your fault. I made everything your fault, even though it rarely was, and lots of times I didn't even need an excuse to be horrible and I'd pick fights with you for no reason at all; I'd be mean and hurtful and ungrateful and I need to say how sorry I am for that.

I look back at those times and I am so ashamed of myself. You've really never been anything other than kind to me and I repaid you by treating you like shit. And I can't make excuses for that; I don't have any and, even if I did, I don't want to – there is no excusing being a moody little teenage nightmare. But I do want to at least try and explain WHY. Why I was only difficult with you, why I snapped at you, why I'd project every bit of shit in my life onto you.

I like to try and hold everything together in my life. I like to be happy around my friends and fun around people I've never met before. Outwardly I don't like to show the world I'm worried about things. In my relationship I want to be sure that I'm getting it right and, as a result, I know that I can't snap at Alex every time he leaves the loo seat up. I spend a large portion of time *totally* bullshitting myself into believing that everything is absolutely peachy, that I'm a GREAT adult and that, as the strong, independent woman you raised me to be, I don't need anybody to help me. But of course we both know that isn't true. In fact, we both know that a lot of the time, much like the rest of the world, I'm only just holding it together. And that's so tiring. It's so tiring being 'up' all the time and being fun all the time.

And so when I ring you or see you and get the chance to just breathe out and relax (because that's the feeling I get when I speak to you), everything I've been holding onto just falls out of me; I can't stop it. The disappointment I feel when someone rejects an idea I've had; the exhaustion I feel after three weeks of burning the candle at both ends; the fact that I missed the bus, lost my glasses and spilt my coffee all over the carpet; the frustration I feel at myself when I'm covered in spots, haven't been to the gym in a year and have left all my work to the very last minute – it's all fine and it doesn't matter, until I speak to you and I'm allowed to not be fine about it for a minute. That's when the onslaught comes. THAT'S why I'm difficult with you and give you a hard time. You've always said to me that we take things out on the people closest to us, and that's why I do it, because you really are the person I am closest to in the whole entire world.

And I am SO lucky for that. I'm so lucky to have you to look up to. You've worked so hard your entire life; you've raised three (smashing) children, you did your first Ironman competition aged fifty and haven't looked back and you've been totally instrumental in starting one of the most incredible charities: Help for Heroes. But more impressive than any of that, you are just the kindest person I know. NOTHING is too much trouble for you; you always have time for a friend in need and I know that you would go to

the ends of the earth for someone you love. Do you have any
idea how incredibly inspirational you are? If I grow up to be
a fraction of the woman you are then I can die happy.

I've given you such a hard time, and I know I can't have
been the easiest daughter to raise, but I need you to know
that I don't take you for granted. I am blindingly aware of
how lucky I am, and I need you to know how much I love
you.

We've had so much fun in our life together, which is
something most people can only dream of doing with
their mums. Ordering Jägerbombs at 10.30 a.m. halfway
up a mountain in Austria to try and beat the hangover
from the night before; having you bunk with Alex and I at
Glastonbury because you got locked out of your Winnebago
at 3 a.m.; running the last 10k of your Ironman together (me
in flip-flops) and fighting with that horrible security guard
who picked me up and removed me from the course. That
time on my tenth birthday when you took me shopping
and bought yourself a pair of shoes with toy fish in the heels
because that was all I wanted for my birthday; our girls'
holiday to China where we teased you ruthlessly for being
so polite about things you quite clearly hated; watching you
wrestle a magnum of champagne off a waiter while dancing
on the bar. But we've also had some hard times together
too – times when we've cried and been sad and have wanted
nothing more than for it to all be over. But the fact that
we've always had each other, through thick and thin, light
and dark? It's more than I could have ever hoped for; it's
made it all possible, all OK.

You joke that when you're old and all of those Ironmans have finally taken their toll I'll end up wiping your arse when one day you won't be able to do it anymore and that's all the payment you need for your incredible generosity with us. I would like to say now, publicly, that it would be an absolute privilege to wipe your bum – one I would be honoured to do.

The blog, the book, would not have been possible without you. Nothing I've ever done or achieved in my life would have been possible without you, and because I don't say it enough: thank you. Thank you for giving me life, giving me support, giving me someone to look up to.

And finally I wanted to end by answering the question that I get asked nearly as much as who my hero is: How did you become such a passionate feminist? Well, how could I not be? My mother is the strongest person I know. She's the one who's proud of me when she finds out that I weed on the side of the road when the boys did (because why should a woman have to wait to find a bathroom?). She's the one who will happily arm-wrestle a man who is trying to pay for her dinner. And that, I suppose, is what I really need to thank you for. For making me into the woman I am today. For teaching me that I should take no shit, for telling me that I could do anything and, above all, for believing in me.

I really don't know what I did to get so lucky, but Jesus, I'm so happy that I did. I love you more than you will ever know.

Em xxx

Dear Me As A Mum

Oh, my God. Have we done it? How was it? Was it agony? Was it gross? I bet it was totally gross. Did you freak out? I reckon you totally freaked out. Or was it actually OK? How did you cope with being pregnant? That is mega. I can't believe we have COOKED a person. Eek! This is insane. Well done. This is 23-year-old you, by the way. Twenty-three years old, very much alarmed by the idea of pregnancy, can't imagine ever being grown-up enough to be a mother . . . that one. Remember me? God, I'm proud of you.

How many are there? What did we have? Did the rumours about twins skipping a generation come true? Do we have twins? Worse, do we have triplets? Please tell me we didn't have triplets. If so, please tell me you've roped in another husband so that we can all have the responsibility of just one each. Are we coping? Are you OK?

Are you literally living in baby sick right now, or are you rocking motherhood chic? (Don't worry, I know we've never *rocked* anything before and that seems like a weird place to start, so I'm cool with baby sick.)

How are you coping without any sleep? Like, seriously. Is it as bad as they say? Because right now I'm struggling to believe that you, future me, is coping on minimal sleep. (I went to bed at 9 p.m. last night and still found 7 a.m. a proper life-or-death-type struggle, so I am NOT looking forward to this.) Are you totally exhausted? (Please say no.)

But WAIT. Rewind again. WHAT DID WE HAVE?! Please tell me we had girls. At least one, please, please, please.

OK, I'm guessing that we did. We better have done; if not, don't you dare tell me you've stopped. Don't you stop until we've got one, you hear me? In my head we already have one, so I'm just going to talk as if we do, OK? Is she alright? Is she happy? She's not being bullied, is she? Wait, hang on, please tell me she's more than happy. Please tell me she is totally MAD. That she's weird and wonderful and brave and confident. Please tell me she's the way her auntie Katya was as a child? Totally incredibly awkwardly fabulous. All the stuff I wish we'd been when we were younger.

Does she let you plait her hair? And dress her all in pink? Or are girls not allowed to wear pink anymore? In 2017 the world seems to be heading in the direction of all this gender-neutral stuff; was that just a fad? Does she like dolls? Please say no. Or at least not the ones that blink and shit themselves, or have they been outlawed too? They're probably sexist, aren't they? I mean, let's face it, who are we as a society to assume that a young girl should know that one day, if she's very very lucky, she will be a mother, eh? Ah fuck it. I know they're sinister, but go and get her one now if she hasn't got one already. Or does she hate all that stuff? Does she eat mud and wear trousers a lot? That's cool too . . . as long as she's happy.

And the boy. Did we have a boy? Is he kind? Please, please, tell me that he is good and kind and he's making you proud.

Does he offer his seat to old women on buses? I hope so, unless that too has been banned on the grounds of sexism? If I had to guess I would assume it has; ask his uncle Finlo to tell him about that time he had his head bitten off by a woman on the bus after he offered her his seat. Chivalry is dying here, how is it with you? As long as he's kind and gentle and lovely and respectful that's all that matters, I suppose.

I so don't want to tell you how to raise our kids. After all, what do I know? Hell, nothing. I found out for the first time the other day that little boys got erections and I laughed until I cried. I have absolutely nothing in the way of authority here, and I'm sure you're doing a swell job on your own, but there is so much that I want to tell you, or to tell our kids, so please, please, pass my messages on to them. There is SO much they need to know and I'm so scared that you've been too busy being tired and stressed and forgetful (because you are the grown-up me, and I know how forgetful I am) to tell them yet.

Where are they right now? First things first, you need to go and find them and give them the biggest cuddle you can muster, and tell them that they are beautiful. And then you need to promise me that you'll make sure to do it again and again until they absolutely believe it. And then tell them a few more times after that, so you can be sure they never ever forget it.

Please make sure you are supportive. I know they'll be driving you bananas right now, but don't forget how much we did the same to our mum . . . or still do in my case (and probably yours)! I know you know this already but I feel the need to remind you that we only did that, or do that, to our lovely mum because we take out everything on the ones closest to us. So don't take their temper tantrums for granted, because it is absolute confirmation of how much they love you. Remember all those times we flew off the handle at Mum? Why did we do it? Because she was our best friend and we were so bloody lucky.

Are our kids your best friends? Please say yes. That's something I dream of, that I am SO excited about. Do you spend enough time with them doing fun stuff? Do you carve out time at weekends? And make them actually talk to you at supper rather than sitting them down with their iPads. Wait. You haven't given them iPads yet, have you? Say no. Or are they a legal requirement for all children across the land now as part of Apple's world domination? Probably.

Do you go to the park? And give them fish and chips on Friday evenings out of the paper? (Those are some of my favourite memories, of sitting in the park on Fridays after school on our way to the chippy.) Have you taught them to ride a bike? Or a HORSE? CAN THEY RIDE HORSES? Are you making sure they are filled to the brim with happy moments that will turn into wonderful memories?

The girls. Are the girls old enough to shop yet? Take them now, after you've read this. Even if they're not. Even if they hate it. Take them to the shops and make it fun. Shopping must always be fun for them, even when nothing fits, because Topshop didn't listen to me and the changing room lighting is the worst thing EVER and it's all bollocks – don't ever let it not be.

Do they have any passions? Please tell me there's some stuff they're really passionate about. Even if it's being a vegetarian, or a vegan, and you never know what to cook for them, please be OK with that. Do they love ballet or are they more into eating earwigs? Let them try everything until they love something. I hate that the only thing anyone seems to be able to tell me about my childhood is how I couldn't say the letter 'C' until I was four. It's not that I need our kids to be more impressive than I was, but I would at least like to explore that avenue for them.

Although, don't let me be pushy. Don't you DARE be pushy. (Yes, I see the irony of the CAPLOCK here.) If the only notable thing about them so far is that they are struggling to say certain letters and have big ears then that's fine, but if they're showing so much as an interest in something let them develop it. Even if it's the art of 'clowning' (which I learned recently is a real thing and has got to be by far the most terrifying thing on the planet). Let their dad deal with that but don't tell them not to.

I am SO excited to BE you and to meet them, you don't even know. Just make sure of a few teensy things for me, will you?

- That they've got good manners. (Good enough that they rival Finlo's infamous incident when he farted and, when asked by a really embarrassed mum, 'What do you say?' he replied with, 'Thank you for having me.' I want it to be THAT embedded in them that politeness is key.)

- That they try their hands at at least one musical instrument. I'm not expecting a miracle, and if they hate it let them stop, but please make them try. Unless it's the violin, because unless they're really bloody good at that (which is unlikely considering how terrible I was) then it's going to be the worst time of our lives. For the sake of our eardrums, don't take that risk. Show them the piano, recorder or guitar instead.

- That every Christmas you'll put them in a ridiculous outfit and make them pose for a proper picture that will get printed (hoping that still happens where you are) and stored for the future. They won't thank you for a good few years but you'll all be grateful for it one day.

- They stay close to their family. Even if Finlo and Katya go on to have the most terrible children in the world, make sure they all hang out because family is the most important thing and they might need them some day.

- Make sure they exercise. And not like in an 'I'm setting you up for an eating disorder' sort of way, but in a 'playing football can be way more fun than watching TV' kind of way.

- That they like reading. I know you can't FORCE that to happen, but surround them with enough books and they may just feel resigned to a lifetime of being intellectually stimulated. Which would be great.

- Listen to all the music with them that we listened to when we were young, but remember not to do as our parents always did and ask every time it comes on the radio: 'How do you even know this song?' They'll know it because you played it to them and you'll put them off ALL old music if you ask them that every time.
- That they have good table manners. Eating with their mouths closed and knife AND fork to be used in the correct hands and no elbows on the table. Oh my God, I've already turned into my mother.
- They can talk to anyone. Small talk gets you a long way in this life and without it you're lost. Help them get that from an early age and you'll literally be able to take them anywhere with you, rather than having to leave them at home with a babysitter to avoid the shame. That was a joke, by the way.
- Teach them to cook. And not just gingerbread cookies and cupcakes. Let them help you with dinners and Sunday lunches. Teach them all about food for me? Please. Lord knows they won't learn it anywhere else.

I know you're going to do all of this anyway. Shoving a human out of your vagina is going to change me but not that much, I know you got this.

The only thing that really, really matters is that they're happy. Please don't take your eye off the ball here, even for a minute. I cannot stress to you how important it is that they are happy. I NEED for them to be proud of themselves, to love themselves, and that is only going to happen with your help and support. Kids need their mums; think about how badly we need ours. Please make sure you are giving it to them by the bucket-load.

You know, the funny thing is, I was never that bothered about the idea of having kids; they were something blurry and far off and something I couldn't really picture happening to me. But writing to you now, the more I think about it, the more excited I am. It's just got to be the greatest feeling in the whole world. I can't wait.

Please keep this letter somewhere safe. I think when I get to where you are I could do with rereading it a few dozen times.

Take care, and look after yourself as well. I almost forgot to say! Have a bath, a drink, a night out, a shag. Whatever it is, DO IT. Look after number one, girl. I can't wait to meet you, and to meet them too.

All my love,

Childless Em xxxx

Dear Emily Aged Seventy

Ahaha, no way are we seventy right now! I can't even deal
with that. How did we get so OLD? (I'm going to keep
talking to you as if you weren't a little old pensioner btw –
by the way ... YOU KNOW THAT ONE! – because I'm
sure that's not what we grew up to be and, if we did, then I
know for sure that you'll need a message from someone cool
and trendy and hip who speaks in acronyms to keep you
young!)

Before I start, though, I've got to ask: ARE WE LIVING
IN THE COMMUNE RIGHT NOW? Did it happen?
Did my friends and I save up our money (/rob a bank) like
we planned and spend it all on a big scary castle somewhere
together? Are you in there now doing all sorts of drugs and
terrorising the local children like we talked about? Please,
please tell me that it happened. If so, how much fun is that?!
I take it the grandkids don't visit much? Or have you made
them totally outrageous and unruly to the point where they
just don't leave anymore?

Is the date set for the huge acid drop that will see the most
shocking pensioner suicide pact in history? Is that still the
plan, because I'm kind of counting on that one; counting
on growing old disgracefully and going out with the biggest
hallucinogenic bang EVER. Ah, I'm kind of kidding, I don't

really care where we ended up, as long as we're happy. Hell, the fact that we're still alive is actually good enough for me.

If I'm honest, a part of me has long since suspected that my generation wouldn't get the chance to grow old because we'd have all been wiped out by our mobile phones and obsession with social media. Either that or Trump would have put his enormous orange foot into something and we'd have ended up pawns in a nuclear war we were destined to lose, but clearly, what do I know? We made it!

There is SO much I want to ask you. God, I wish you could write back; mind you, you've probably forgotten how to do that now, since I suspect pens were probably outlawed in 2035 along with paper and stamps. I feel like I'm looking into a time machine, or at least talking into one, and it's exciting me more than I can say. But seriously, I've got to know, how did we do? We had babies. How are they? Did they have babies yet? That blows my MIND. Me as a granny, I can't imagine it! Did we get married? More importantly, did we STAY married? Or did we end up doing it more than once (if so, what was the etiquette: two big white dresses? I've wanted to ask people who have been married more than once but it always seemed rude).

What happened to this book? Did people read it? Did we do another one? And Pretty Normal Me? Are you still running it? Rocking #nomakeupselfies every night? Please say yes and be the most gangster seventy-year-old in town. Finlo and Katya, how are they? Still winding you up and nicking your make-up? (Obviously that last bit is meant for Katya, unless Fin turned to drag in his twilight years, of course.) How's our health been? Did all those years of fun-free dieting pay off? Or was it all a waste of time? Liver packed in yet, or did it survive the years of abuse we inevitably gave it? Ah, I'm confident that he handled it OK.

Actually, I have a better question: what state is the world in right now? It's at times like this that I'm actually grateful you can't write back. I'm not sure I want to hear the answers if planet earth follows the course it's on as I write this letter.

(Just to refresh your memory, here's a snapshot of the world circa 2017: the war in the Middle East is breaking my heart. Syria is being torn apart and World War Three is actually looking imminent, judging by North Korea's behaviour. The migrant crisis is at its worst so far and it seems there just isn't the space for all these people in Europe, either that or the government are being total twats; I think it's a bit of both. The whole of Europe is on terrorist watch, not unsurprisingly considering attacks are happening at least once every six months at the moment and plots are being foiled hundreds of times a day, or so MI5 suggests. I think the Russians are up to something but it's hard to know for sure. Donald Fucking Trump is now the President of the United States; I have no words other than: I'm scared. The UK decided to leave the EU last year; I don't know why and no one knows yet if it's a good thing or a bad thing. I suppose we'll have to wait and see.

Last year everyone legendary and amazing died; don't know why but it was horrid and meant that 2016 was basically the worst year ever. Mental health issues are the words on everyone's lips but no one is actually doing an

awful lot about them; they're still not explained properly
and more people than ever are suffering with them, current
statistics suggest one in four. We're social media obsessed
but people haven't yet quite got the hang of using it like
the decent human beings they probably are. There's a lot of
trolling going on and quite a lot of the older generation are
understandably weary and frightened of it in equal measure.

Feminism has come on leaps and bounds but sexism is still
rife; I still regularly get shouted at from moving vans and
the battle for equal pay continues. Models still look critically
thin and clothes are not being made to fit the average size
of women in the UK, which at the present time is a 16. The
plus size movement is good but for every curvy woman I
see in a campaign I'll see ten more magazine covers telling
me how I can BLAST MY BODY FAT, so I don't think it's
good enough yet.

At the time of writing we have a female prime minister
again, which is great, but we didn't actually vote for her
(although we might have done by the time this book is
published) so I'm not sure I can comment on a breakthrough
in society yet because we didn't get a choice in it.

Everyone has diabetes, no one can afford anything and
house prices are way too high. The NHS is at breaking
point and there's no money for anything. There's crap phone
signal pretty much everywhere, trains are always running
late and every other motorway in the country is undergoing
road works. Animals are facing extinction everywhere
because we're greedy bastards who are killing them for
sport; seriously, someone shot a gorilla last year. The ones

that aren't getting shot are in trouble too, though. We keep chopping their houses down to make room for more human houses and to get wood and palm oil. The ice caps are melting and that's our fault; the whole world is polluted to shit because we are incredibly wasteful in every element of our lives and there are more people living on the streets then you would believe . . . basically, it's all a bit shit.

So here's hoping it got better. It must have got better, right? There's no way on earth that it could have got worse and, honestly, if it has please don't tell me because I truly don't think I could deal with that. If it does, then I might just have to stay here. Since you can't write back I suppose it'll just have to be a surprise. (I will keep my fingers crossed, though.)

What are you up to? Are you still working or have you retired now? If that's the case you'd better not just be sitting on your arse; with all that time on your hands I'm praying to God that you're filling your days with loads of really great, important, meaningful stuff. By that I hope you know that I do NOT mean just visiting your friends under the pretence of 'helping the elderly' – that does NOT count. Fifty quid says that's what you've been doing. I know you too well. If you're currently thinking, Oh shit, now I owe her £50, then I'll let you off if you can just get up and out and do something useful. Nothing makes you happier than doing things you love, or at least it does at the moment, so I hope you're keeping that up. If not, let this be the shove you need to get you going again.

Have you started hoarding? This is my biggest fear. I bet you have. Oh GOD, have we been approached by one of those *Hoarder Next Door* television programmes yet? You're cringing aren't you? Aha, I knew it. Are we the house that all the neighbours avoid for fear of catching cluttery-itus? You've probably still got the very laptop that I'm writing this on. Hidden underneath every other technological gadget that you've used in the last fifty years, which will be thousands. Oh well, I suppose it's not worth stopping now, and it's the ultimate 'screw you' to your kids, isn't it? Leaving all of your worthless junk for them to go through. Here's hoping we can rival Granny's attempts when Mum found a tin of soup in her cupboard after she died in 2000 that had gone off in 1960 or something. Good to keep tradition alive.

Have you travelled the world yet? IF NOT THEN FOR GODSAKE GO AND TRAVEL THE WORLD RIGHT NOW. By the time we hit 71 I'm expecting to have gone to Egypt, the Maldives, Hong Kong, Australia, Argentina, Brazil, and driven across America. Please don't let me down as I really have got my heart set on that stuff.

Assuming we have grandkids, are you spoiling them? The answer better be yes, because as far as I can see, that's the whole point of a grandparent. Too many sweeties, lots of toys and no set bedtimes. I know you'll be doing that already but keep it up, please; never stop spoiling them.

Oh, I don't know. I don't know anything. You got it, girl, you're seventy, you've got forty-five-odd years on me; I won't insult you by telling you how to live your life.

There's just one thing I want to check. I want to check that you're still surrounded by people who you love and who love you. I want to check that you never let your friendships slip away or held a grudge about something you should've let go. I want to check that where your friends are concerned you haven't been short-sighted because the ones surrounding me now are so truly wonderful that if you've fucked it up I'll bloody kill you. In a letter I wrote to them, I said I never wanted to live with regret and I meant that. I just hope that you haven't forgotten it and, if you have, then remember it's never too late to make it right. If there's one thing I know for sure it's that there's always time for that.

God, I hope we've had a good one. I'm sure we have. It's so funny to think of myself as old, I never thought I'd see the day. In truth, I never thought I would grow old; maybe it's because my ego is too big and I was always told that only the good die young, or maybe it's because I didn't want to get my hopes up but, either way, I'm pleased we made it.

It's so funny to think now, as I sit in a house that I don't understand, with bills to pay to companies I can't remember the names of, and with odd socks on, that one day I will grow up. That one day I'll have to stop saying 'When I'm an adult I want to be . . .' and calling my mum to ask her for help when I can't open the washing machine door. It's funny to think of myself with a life, and life experiences, and it's funny to think of it all ending. Morbid, I know, but it's funny when you think about it. Because when you're young you think you're going to live forever, don't you? That's the assumption. And I'm young now, so that's my assumption.

'I'll quit smoking when I'm older.' 'I'll stop drinking when I have kids.' 'I'll exercise the day that pigs fly.' All big promises for a future we just assume we're going to have. And in my case I hope we have because there really is so much I want to do with my life.

But writing this letter, writing this whole book, has made me realise life is so damn precious. I'm sure you'll be sitting there now reading this letter and laughing at my naïvety, feeling like you've been going on forever. But even now I can see how fast my life is going and it's scaring me that I can't slow it down. Each day the sun rises, just as the day before, and we think nothing of it until one day we look up and realise it's Christmas again, it's our birthday again, and suddenly we're old; suddenly we're seventy.

I hope we had a blast, I really do. I hope we made each second count. I hope that we never took anything for granted, that we continued to love with all our heart, that we continued to dance like an absolute lunatic, that we smiled until it hurt and laughed until we cried. I hope that we trusted unconditionally and forgave quickly. I hope that we never stopped singing and drinking and snogging (although not all at the same time). I hope we stopped rushing and found the time to appreciate things. And I hope we chose happiness every time. I hope more than anything that we chose happiness.

All I can do now, I suppose, is trust myself and trust in the world that, by the time I get to you, everything will be OK. That I will have created happy children and remained a good friend; that in dedicating my life to this project, to Pretty Normal Me, that I will have made a difference, however small, to someone, somewhere. All I can do now is trust.

There is nothing left for me to say or do now other than to promise you that I will love and cry and smile and dance and sing and LIVE, and I will not waste a moment of it.

I want to promise you that I will start getting out of bed earlier and meditating before breakfast. I want to promise you that I will start moisturising my skin and taking better care of my hair and I want to promise you that I will keep in reasonably good physical shape so as to protect my knees when I'm older, but you know me and you know that I can't promise those things. I can try, but I can't *promise* them, I'm too hopeless. What I can promise you though is that I will not take my life for granted and that I'll do my best to make each second count. I promise you that whenever I can I will live in the moment. I will say yes to more things and I will open my heart and mind to more experiences. I promise you I will do the best I can.

You'll forgive me for saying that I *can* wait to meet you; while it will be nice to see quite how wrinkly we get, I've got a fair amount to get through before that and so, if it's alright with you, I'll stay here for as long as I possibly can.

I didn't say it enough to you when you were younger and for that I'm sorry, but I love you, old girl, thanks for being great. It's been an honour and a privilege working with you.

Hang in there.

Em xxxx